TO: ~~[illegible]~~

God m[illegible]

Keep Haiti in prayer.

Sis Dollie 2016

The Rebellious Missionary: My Years as a Medical Missionary in Haiti

by Dollie Bennett-Milfort

edited by Kathleen Grimm Garrett

ISBN: 978-1-329-52954-0

This book is dedicated to the Haitian people, especially the women.

Thanks to Bailey Temple Church of God in Christ and all those who kept me in their prayers. Thank you to my family for allowing me to go to Haiti year after year. Special thanks to Bishop Carlis Moody and his wife for buying me my first vehicle in Haiti.

This book is also in memory of Dr. Mary Lou Belvin and my husband.

1:
Haiti: Location and Climate

"Ayati" (Haiti) as the original inhabitants named it, means "a land of mountains." Haiti is three fourths mountains. There is nowhere you can stand in Haiti and not see a mountain. There are two main mountains in Haiti. One mountain is called Chaine du Haut Piton, or "chain of mountains," which is the largest mountain. The Chaine de le Selle is the other. Christopher Columbus was the first European to discover Haiti in 1492. When he arrived he also saw Arowak Indians, the original inhabitants of the island. Columbus called the island "La Isla Espanola," Spanish for "The Spanish Island."

Haiti is located in the Caribbean chain of islands, east of Cuba, south of the Bahamas, and north of Jamaica. Haiti is about 623 square miles. Haiti has a tropical climate. The average temperature is between 80-100 degrees in Port-au-Prince, the capital. The summer months, June-October, are the hottest. In Kenscoff, a city north of Port-au-Prince, very high in the mountains, the temperature ranges from about 60-80 degrees. The elevation in Kenscoff is 4000 feet. Here, far up in the cold mountains, the soil is red, just like in Georgia, where I was born. It can get cold in the winter months, November through January. The temperatures can drop to about 40 degrees. The people living in these regions sometimes wear heavy clothes and the rich use fireplaces to heat their homes.

Haiti has a population of over 7 million people; about 95% of Haitians are of African descent. The remaining 5% are biracial. The colonizing French had children by black Haitians. Some Haitians are Arabic and some are white. The biracial population makes up about one half of the country's elites. Haiti's biracial population mainly belongs to the middle and upper classes. They are doctors, lawyers, or merchants. Many received their education in France, and most of them live in modern houses. In Haiti, you have the biracial elites, and then you have the black educated elites. They are the ones who really control Haiti; they are the old money.

The official language is French, but the only ones who can read, write and speak it are the elites, which is less than 25%. Everyone speaks Creole. For years, the spelling of Creole was always in flux. It was often based on phonetics. Speakers guessed on the sound and went from there. Creole became an official language in 1987. Prior to that Creole was considered a dialect.

About 80% of Haiti's people are Roman Catholic, many of them combining African Animism called Voodoo into their religious beliefs and ceremonies. Other religious groups include Baptist, about 10%; Pentecostals, 4%, and Adventists, about 1%.

Haiti got its independence from France in 1804. A slave revolt led by Toussaint Louverture began in 1801. Louverture was later captured by the French and died in a French prison. The following leader, Jean

Jacques Dessaline, declared Haiti to be the first Black independent country in the Western hemisphere. In 1806 Dessaline was assassinated, and so began the violent history of Haiti.

Haiti's economy has been shrinking since the early 1980s while the population continues to grow. In 1996, Haiti's per capita gross for domestic product was $360. This put Haiti among the world's poorest nations. It is the poorest country in the Western hemisphere. About 75% of the work force is unemployed. Haiti's debt is $1 billion.

Haitian farmers typically work two acre plots of land. They raise barely enough food to feed their families. Their main crops usually include beans, corn, rice, and yams. Some are fortunate enough to own livestock like chickens, goats and pigs. They mainly live in small, one- room huts with thatched roofs and walls constructed of dried, mud-covered sticks. This is in the rural areas of Haiti where most of the people live. In the larger cities, they have homes built out of concrete blocks. Of course, the wealthy live very well, in nicer homes.

Haiti has no mining because whatever minerals are left, are unusable. They do have limestone, clay, salt, and some copper. Haiti manufactures only small handicrafts, some baseball cover stitching, and beading on clothes. Most of the factories, of which there are less than 10, are foreign-owned.

Haiti's severe deforestation has limited the value of forest products. The constant cutting down of trees for fuel and the resulting soil erosion have led to this issue.

Other than private generators, the Pèligre hydroelectricity plant on the Artibonite River is the only source of commercial energy. In 1996 Pèligre only produced 415 kilowatts per hour. Most of Haiti's poor use charcoal for fuel and cooking.

Haiti's roads were built by the U.S. marines during the U.S. occupation of Haiti from 1915-1934. Of the 2585 miles of road, only about one quarter is paved. Even the main roads are in poor condition, and most bridges have become unusable.

The country has one international airport in Port-au-Prince, recently named after its first leader, Toussaint Louverture.

Of Haiti's population of seven million plus, 65% live in poverty. Their average income is about $1 a day, less than $400 a year. Only 51% ever attend primary school. About 35-40% of the adult population cannot read or write. Some don't know how old they are. Life expectancy is 52 years of age. The infant mortality rate is 100 in every 1000 births. Diseases, especially infections, are at an all-time high. AIDS, Tuberculosis, Hepatitis, Malaria, and intestinal parasites are very common. Haiti's medical system is struggling to cope with the nation's serious health issues. There is only one physician for every 10,855 inhabitants, and medical facilities are poor.

2:
The Call

Many people have asked me "How did you find yourself going to Haiti?" It is at this point that I tell them of "The Call." I had been a captain in the U.S. Army Reserves Nurse Corps for a number of years, and a Home Health Care Nurse. Nursing had been a big part of my life for quite some time. In 1980 I had the opportunity to visit Europe with a dear friend of mine, Sue. She and I were both nurses who worked for Visiting Nurses Association of America, an association that advocates for home care nursing to the sick. My friend and I both worked in the inner city of Detroit. Even though we were great friends, we were also opposites in many ways. She is very soft-spoken and reserved, and I am very out-spoken and independent. She is White and I am Black. She was divorced and I, at the time, was married. I was also Sue's immediate supervisor, and so when she invited me to go with her on a trip to Denmark, to a Nurses Christian Fellowship Conference, many people did not think it was going to work out, but it did! My husband Ronald agreed to look after our three children: Allida, 13, Gwenae 14, and Tony, 16. Sue planned the three week trip. She taught me how to pack all my clothes for the three weeks in a travel shoulder bag, and arranged that we stay at pensions (homes shared with families) wherever we traveled. Sue and I left Detroit in June of 1980, bound for Europe. I had no idea that this trip would forever change my life.

After touring Germany and Austria for two weeks, we headed to Denmark. The night before we were to catch the morning train to Denmark, I had a dream. This is what I dreamed: I dreamed that God asked me to be a missionary in a foreign country. I told Him I did not want to do this because all the missionaries that I had seen that lived in Africa came home looking thin and malnourished, and they always told sad stories about starving children dying in the bush, or how they had to eat bugs and strange animals to survive. I told God that after listening to these missionaries, I felt sad and guilty and often, when I did not eat all of my food. I thought I could hear the missionaries say "Some child would gladly eat the food we throw in the trash." In the dream I told God "That's not for me. Just let me be a regular Christian and help people here in the good old USA!" But then I remembered who I was talking to. It was God who forgave me all my sins and accepted me as one of His children. I felt I owed Him my life. But wait, I thought, there might be an out. I thought I should be sure it was Him who was speaking to me. I told Him He had to prove to me that this was Him I was talking to and not just myself. That is when my first dream immediately turned into another dream, this time with a test.

In this dream I was running with Sue to catch the train for Denmark. She was in front of me. As I was running I heard footsteps behind me running as well. The person behind me was a tall, Black man and looked like he was from Arica. He tapped me on the shoulder and startled me. He began speaking to me in a foreign language. I did not understand him, so I just smiled and that is when he said in accented English he thought I was a Nigerian woman he knew. He apologized and walked away. At the time I saw no connection between these two dreams.

When I woke the next morning, I shared the dreams with Sue who brushed them off as typically strange dreams. We left the pension after eating our breakfast of cheese, sweet rolls, juice and coffee, and headed to the train station. We were running a little late, so we hurried knowing that European trains run on time. If the train stated it would leave the station at 7:59 am, you had better be on it! As I was running I heard someone in back of me running. All of a sudden the person got right on my tracks and I stopped. A man of African descent began to speak to me in a foreign language. I smiled at him to tell him I didn't understand what he was saying. Immediately he began to speak in a heavy accent. "Excuse me Miss. I thought you were a woman of my country, of Nigeria. You look like someone I know." I said "No," and smiled again. He turned and walked away. I didn't realize what had just happened until Sue brought it to my attention. It was the dream. It all happened just like in my dream! It was then I understood that I had been called. Both Sue and I cried realizing what had just happened.

When I returned home after three weeks in Europe and my extraordinary dreams, I had feelings of both joy and sadness. I explained to my husband and children what God had done. I told them about my dreams and what had happened to me at the train station in Denmark. Ronald just looked at me and laughed. My children didn't have much to say. I went to my church and told my pastor and several church members who all laughed, rolled their eyes and asked "Did God tell you where you are going? What language you will speak? What about your family? What about your job?" I next confided in my sister Annie Ruth. She was the one who raised me after our mother died when I was eight. She was like a mother to me. She said "Dollie, are you sure this is what God wants for you?" I told her "Yes. I am very sure."

To the questions about my family, my job, where I was going or how, I had no answers. All I knew was that God had called me to go somewhere and spread the Gospel. I was sure God was going to send me to Africa, maybe Ghana. At the Nurses' Christian Fellowship Conference in Denmark, I met Christine, a Christian nurse from Ghana who had invited me to visit her and her family. Her husband was a chicken farmer in Ghana and quite wealthy. I thought God would send me there and I wouldn't be hungry and could live quite well. I also thought God could save my husband Ronald. Ronald went to church and he was a great singer, but he never practiced being a Christian. He had had many affairs during our marriage, and before I accepted Christ, we had many physical fights. I stopped physically fighting with Ronald after I became a Christian, but he continued to be verbally abusive. We had a rough marriage, but I believed that God was going to change Ronald's heart. I thought we would be like other missionary families, you know, the husband and wife and their children all preaching and singing the Gospel to some heathens somewhere. Well, soon enough I was reminded of the phrases "My thoughts are not your thoughts" and "Make your plans in pencil because God has the eraser."

In 1983, three years after my trip to Europe, I still had not gone anywhere. No one asked me to Africa, and my husband was still not a Christian. My son Tony was 18 years old and finished with high school. I gave him the option to work, go to college or join the military. He did not find a job, and did not want to go to college, so I took him to the recruiting office in downtown Detroit and he joined the military. That same year my husband left me. We were still married, but Ronald had a girlfriend at work whom he had promised to marry. He had told her we were already divorced. I still believed in God though, and I still believed that somehow or someway I was going to Africa and Ronald was going to be a Born Again Believer.

About three months later, in September of that year, I got a call from my mother-in-law saying my husband was in the hospital. He had suffered a massive brain hemorrhage from an aneurysm, but he was still alive. When I arrived at the hospital, I asked to speak to the doctor. The neurosurgeon showed me the x-ray of my husband's brain. The surgeon told me one aneurysm had ruptured, and three remained. Ronald's blood pressure was over 300. He was too unstable to operate on. I immediately began to pray: "God save my husband's life and soul." I still believed that God was going to save my husband, but when I walked into Mt. Carmel Hospital, I heard God speak to me. He stated that He was delivering me, setting me free, like a bird out of a cage. It was then I knew Ronald was not going to live. Ronald was on a breathing machine and non-responsive. They took him to ICU, and there I stayed with him for six days. I whispered in Ronald's ear that I had forgiven him. Later in the week the three other aneurysms ruptured. On the fifth day he was declared brain dead and he died the next day. He never regained consciousness.

There I was: 35 years old, a widow, a son in the army, and two teenage daughters who were giving me the blues. The oldest, Gwenae, had a boyfriend who was selling drugs. His name was simply, Man. She had moved in with him and later had two children by him. Allida, my youngest, was skipping school and going to her sister's house to hang out. Did God forget about me? Did I misunderstand? Was the Nigerian man in the train station just a coincidence? I had so many questions, but no answers.

I buried my husband in October, 1983. In November of that same year, I attended a National Church Convention in Memphis, Tennessee. While there as an official of my church, Supervisor Mary Lou Belvin of Detroit asked me "Do you want to go to Haiti with me and Missionary Mary Jane Walton in January?" Without hesitation, I said "Yes!" I had no idea where Haiti was, who the people were, what language they spoke, nothing. I just said "Yes!" And so it was just three months later, in January, 1984 when I first came to the land of Ayati, the poorest country in the Western Hemisphere.

3:
Cite Soleil

When I landed at the international airport in Port-au-Prince, people were riding donkeys and mules. The odor was horrendous. It was hot and dusty. Several houses around the airport were not finished. Neither were several buildings. The women wore scarves with long skirts. The children ran around begging, some had clothes on, some had no clothes on at all. I thought it a horrible place. I stayed for one week, happy to return back to my home in Detroit.

Mom and baby in front of their stick and clay hut. The clay is mixed with water and cement if it's available, spread onto the stick frame, and then allowed to dry in the sun. Many homes are made of clay in the rural areas like L'Attalaye.

A few months later, I was again asked by Mother Mary Lou Belvin if I would go to Haiti to help with a new apartment complex that had been built in Cite Soleil. It needed painting and general physical work. Since no opportunity for me to go to Ghana had come up, I figured I would make the trip to Haiti again. This time I was there for over a week. My aversion to Haiti did not change. My belief that God intended for me to go Ghana to spread His word had also not changed. It was 1986, and again I had a dream. This time, God was much more direct. He simply said "Go to Haiti." Again, I was my stubborn self. I was determined to go to Ghana, and so when I returned from Haiti the second time, I wrote my friend Christine telling her I wished to come and help spread the Gospel in Ghana. I told her that I was willing to go any time just as soon as I heard from her. I had seen photos of her home in Ghana and it was beautiful. In Ghana she was quite wealthy and I longed to spread God's word in such a beautiful, comfortable place. I again bargained with God saying "If Christine does not write back, I will go to Haiti." I figured the odds were against God because Christine was a very faithful letter writer. To this day, I have not heard from Christine. Finally, that same year, 1986, I gave in. I said to myself, "This can't be where God is sending me!" Oh, but it was. I didn't like Haiti. It was so poor and underdeveloped. I could not speak the language. I learned that they got their independence in 1804, but it looked as though time had stood still since that point. What a dump, I thought. Was God sure this is where I should go? I resisted for two years, but I returned to Ayati, to Haiti, finally accepting God's call.

Before I left, I notified my church and my church's Supervisor of Women in Haiti, that God had sent me to Haiti. I needed help with donations of money and medicine for the clinic I was asked to staff. I asked my church family and my friends in the community. I called my church's supervisor in Haiti, but she not only did not grant me permission to go, she wouldn't provide any support for my mission. I told her that God had told me to go to Haiti. She replied that God had not told her, so He couldn't have told me. So, without my church's support, I went. "You can't go to Haiti under the church's banner," the Supervisor told me. So I said to her, "I will go under the banner of Jesus." I was then that the Supervisor of Haiti labeled me as "the Rebellious Missionary." She sent letters to the other churches and to the Bishop of the church in Haiti telling all of them that my mission in Haiti was not sanctioned by the church and that I was a rebellious missionary and they should not accept me. In the meantime, Pastor Joseph Abraham Milfort from Haiti had visited a church where my sister's friend was a Pastor. Elder Henderson told Pastor Milfort about me and thought maybe I could help him with the clinic in a slum of Port-au-Prince. Pastor Abraham had also come against the wishes of his church and had found no one to help him with his clinic. I was the only one willing to go, and this time I went to stay.

Cite Soleil is in the heart of Port-au-Prince. The name means "Sun City," but the best way to describe it is to say it is the most impoverished, densely populated slum in Haiti. There are no trees. There are thousands of poor people who have come from the mountains to look for work and to live. Houses are built from any material that can be found, such as tin sheets, cardboard, wood scraps, and some concrete blocks. People are everywhere! Over 200,000 people live in this small, concentrated area. There are hardly any toilet facilities; people generally defecate in the water, and raw sewage often is seen floating in the streets. People ride donkeys, walk, and pull or push carts loaded with blocks, sugar cane, and other items too heavy to carry. The people sit outside in the sun selling whatever they have, just to make enough to buy food for the day. The smell is indescribable, unlike anything I had ever smelled.

I arrived in Sun City in June, 1986. I had no idea what awaited me. Pastor Abraham's two daughters met me at the airport. I would be working with Milfort and his family. They needed a nurse to help run the clinic in Cite Soleil. When I arrived in Cite Soleil, Milfort was being evicted from his house. We all had to find another place to live. I was shocked, but I believed that since God had sent me there, somehow He would take care of the situation. Milfort found an empty cement building with two rooms and three windows, and that is where we stayed. It was a cement block house. Milfort, his children, mother and others all slept in one room. There was only one mattress, and they let me sleep on it. That first night, when they closed the door to the cement building, I breathed heat. The heat was so intense I could hardly breathe at all, and when I did inhale, I smelled the stench of sewage off the Caribbean Ocean. There were lizards everywhere – on the ceiling, the floor, even the windows. Every time I saw a lizard I jumped, and so did they. As I lay on the mattress in this inferno of a house with lizards crawling everywhere and the stench of feces and urine in my nostrils, I said "Lord, did you really send me here?" And then I thought to myself, "Girl, you are not going to make it. You are going to die down here."

I prayed that night that God would take away the nausea and remove my fear of the lizards. I laid awake for hours, listening to the blaring Creole music I didn't understand. Finally, I slept. When I awoke, I saw another lizard on the wall. When the lizard jumped, I didn't. I then inhaled a deep breath, and to my amazement, I was no longer nauseated and the stench didn't bother me. God had done it one more time! He had removed my resistance.

A typical outdoor kitchen with a recho or grill in Cite Soleil.

People cooked outside on small grills they called "rechos." The rechos are small, round tin circles like containers on three steel legs, about 24 inches high, and the people fill them with charcoal. The women cook their meals of beans and rice, or whatever they can buy, on top of the recho. Food was scarce because no one had much money. Sometimes people would get up early in Cite Soleil because only so many could sleep in a one or two room building, so some had to walk to a friend's home. Some got up early to sell their merchandise or to go to Port-au-Prince to sell. At the crack of dawn the people of Cite Soleil rose. Roosters crowed at 4 am every morning, cars, chugged down the streets. There was never a time in Cite Soleil when there was quiet. There were just so many people moving, and talking, and often just doing nothing

At this time in Haiti, there was much political unrest. President Jean-Claude Duvalier had just left and

Cite Soleil was in political turmoil. Gunshots could be heard night and day. There were days when we would see dead bodies lying in the streets, shot by the military. Because the sun was so hot, the bodies would be swollen and reek. Sometimes dogs would have eaten parts of the bodies. Often the people would cover the bodies with large palm tree leaves. There were days when the shooting got so bad, Milfort and his family and I would have to run to the tops of cement buildings and lie down to stay out of the way of bullets.

On days when it was quiet, I would go into schools or church buildings and see to the sick. Even though I could not yet speak the language, Milfort spoke English and he would translate for me. Most people called him Pastor Abraham. I, however, had started to call him Milfort, yet another way that the people saw that I was different. I did not really want to do any nursing, however. I wanted to preach the Gospel to these poor people and I sincerely hoped that they would accept my Jesus and leave their gods alone. I could not speak Creole or French, and I didn't understand the culture of the Haitian people, and yet there I was, expecting them to accept my God and my culture. I had so much to learn!

4:

Living in Cite Soleil

Never had I seen so many malnourished and dying children. The children had so many rashes on them that I could not find an inch of clear skin. These children were suffering, starving, and often dying. Pregnant women who were eight months pregnant looked more like they were five months pregnant. They too were full of sores and skin rashes, which was more than likely syphilis.

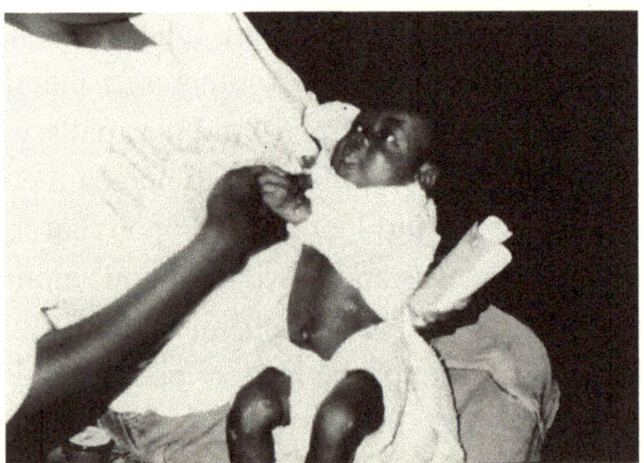

The clinic had no testing equipment to identify the rash covering this baby. Pain relief was given and an anti-itch cream. The baby died soon after this photo was taken, of an unknown rash.

Daily I was seeing 50-60 people in our small clinic with no breeze or relief from the heat. I could not speak the language, but the children of Cite Soleil began to help me. In spite of all the poverty, sickness, and death, the people were friendly. Death was common and suffering a daily companion, but they accepted me and taught me their language and culture with patience and some amusement.

Here I am at the clinic in St. Michel, 1984.

Cite Soleil was so crowded it was difficult to keep myself clean. The children were always in need of a bath. Water was scarce and therefore precious. What water there was had to be purchased. Usually we could get a five gallon bucket filled for 20 cents. Someone who had a hose or large container would see to those who had no water. I remember many days when I only had a cup of water to wash up with. Can you imagine only having a cup of water to wash up with? Well, that's all I had, but the young girls taught me that I should just wash the important areas. Washing one's hair was a luxury. They did have a public shower, but you had to pay a dime to use it. The shower was simply a place that was closed in by tin sheets, and you poured water over yourself. You dried yourself with a towel used by several other people. I know it sounds disgusting, but to me it was great just to have cold water poured over me!

My clothes drying quickly in the hot sun.

Once, when I desperately needed something to drink, the children helped the best way they could. I knew as an RN and Public Health Nurse that the water had to be boiled 10-15 minutes and then cooled and strained before I could drink it. Even then it didn't taste good, and I could see the residue of bacteria in it. If you're really thirsty, though, you'll drink it. This time I was so thirsty I couldn't wait so the children brought me a soda. They brought it to me with their dirty hands and I thought to myself, "They could have TB, HIV, and look at some of them! Some of them have noses running with thick green secretion from who knows which infectious disease so common in Haiti." I did not want to take this drink from their dirty hands which they wiped their noses with. But I was so thirsty! I needed to drink something, so I asked God to help me. I took the bottle, wiped the top and drank the warm cola. I never got sick, not even for a day. I never got diarrhea or even stomach cramps. God, once again, took care of me. God had a lot of lessons for me to learn in Haiti, starting in Cite Soleil.

Once when I was in Cite Soleil, I was sitting by the ocean. It wasn't the pretty, blue Caribbean Ocean people usually think of when they imagine the Caribbean, but a trashy, smelly, feces floating, dark black ocean. I was feeling very depressed, feeling like this was not where I wanted to be. It was one of those days I would ask myself, "Dollie, what are you doing here? You could be home working as an RN, making good money, driving your nice ear, eating at any restaurant, taking a nice bath, sitting in air-conditioning, but here you sit!" I thought I had lost my mind and that no one in Haiti cared about me. It was during these times that I asked God for reassurance that He sent me here, to Haiti. I asked God for a sign that He was hearing me. I looked up at the one beautiful place, the sunny sky and I asked God to make the cloud go away and leave only the sun remaining. God did it, just as I asked! The cloud left! I still wasn't satisfied, though. I asked God to let the cloud reappear in front of the sun. He did it again! Then I was reassured that I was where I was supposed to be, here in Cite Soleil, the smelly, hot, poverty-stricken slums of Port-au-Prince. With sickness and death all around, I was supposed to be here. Just as I thought this, two Haitian men with Bibles came along. They spoke to me in Creole, which I still did not understand. Then they opened their Bibles and pointed to St. Jean 3:16: "For God so loved the world that He gave His Only Son, that whosoever believed in Him shall be saved." I did not know it in Creole, but I recognized "St. Jean" as St. John in my Bible. They kept speaking to me in Creole, and amazingly I felt encouraged even though I had no idea what they were saying. I later thought that maybe they were angels sent by God to encourage me.

Most of the people in Cite Soleil are hungry most of the time. The people are very thin and malnourished, and so was I! I was eating only one or one and a half meals a day. Meat was scarce, so we ate mostly beans, rice, vegetables and occasionally chicken. But the chickens were not like the chickens I was used to. These chickens were not fat and plump like we buy in our stores. These were very skinny chickens with little meat that was very tough, but when the women got through frying it and making tomatoes, onions, and gravy, it was like eating a big steak! Sometimes all of us would buy a sugar cane stick and suck on that for the taste of sweetness. Sometimes Milfort's mother would make a mixture of flour and water with sugar and we would eat that before going to sleep. It tasted very good because it was sweet. It was thick and sweet and we often ate it for supper. This was a common dish for anyone lucky enough to get the ingredients in Cite Soleil. Never say what you won't eat or drink until you really do get hungry. After three months I had lost 30 pounds. I was not sick, but there was simply little food and I had no money to get any more. I was completely dependent on Milfort and his family's generosity.

Cite Soleil sometimes brought back memories of growing up in rural Georgia. We were so poor when I was growing in Columbus, Georgia that sometimes when we found orange and banana peels on the road, we would blow the dirt and bugs off and eat them. Living in Cite Soleil also reminded me of the heat in Georgia and how I could only bathe on wash day after my mother had washed all the clothes. In Georgia, women washed the clothes in a tin tub using very strong soap. When they were finished, all the children took their weekly bath! I remember too going to the outhouse to use the toilet. Yes, God chooses wisely. Little did I realize that growing up in Georgia would prepare me for my life in Haiti. It is amazing how God plans our lives!

5:

The Value of a Penny

What's a penny worth? In the States I used to see them lying on the ground, and I would step over them. I often thought if I thought of them at all, "It's only a penny." After my experience in Haiti, however, my whole concept of pennies changed. 1986 was a very violent year in Haiti. The military was in charge of the country. There were shootings, kidnappings and killings daily. Often people were burned alive, screaming and hollering with kerosene-soaked, burning rubber tires around their necks. This was the era of Jean-Claude, or "Baby Doc" Duvalier's violent regime which was overthrown, replaced by a violent, military-lead regime. It was a chaotic, violent time in Haiti when dead, dismembered bodies in the streets were not an usual sight.

One day I left the slum of Cite Soleil and went downtown to Port-au-Prince. I needed to go to the main telephone company which was called Teleco. I needed to make a collect call home to the United States. At that time in Haiti most people did not have telephones. If anyone needed to call outside the country, they would have to go to Teleco. The government owned Teleco. Teleco was in a building that housed many phones that were inside individual booths. There was no air conditioning, just ceiling fans blowing hot air. When the temperature outside was between 90-100 degrees, you can imagine how hot it was inside the building. Inside the booths you'd sweat profusely.

Public transportation is a flatbed truck with sides the owner of the truck built on and decorated. There are no seats. Riders pay a fare and load on until there truly is no more room.

The process to call was this: You took a number and waited. A person behind a stall would eventually call your number, you'd walk up to the stall and they would ask what country you needed to call. You would then give them the number and they would tell you to sit back down and wait until the phone rang in one of the booths. Once you were called to the booth, an operator from the US would ask for your number. The operator would then call for you and ask the person on the other end if they would accept a collect call from Haiti. If the person refused, you simply went home or tried to call another person. Sometimes I would be in Teleco for hours.

The people I would call were my family, mostly my sister, my church, or friends who said to call if I ever needed money. There was so much turmoil in Port-au-Prince at the time, and the connection was so poor, that it was difficult to call home. After many attempts to reach home without success, I left the building to return to Cite Soleil.

At the time, the fee to ride local transportation, or "Tap Tap," a flat- bed truck with no seats, was fifteen cents for two of us. Money was very difficult for me at this time because all the money I had when I came to Haiti was gone. Usually when I called home, someone would send me some money, but this time I could not reach anyone. When I first came to Haiti, I promised myself "I will never be in a foreign country without any money." I had to eat those words many times over. Sometimes God has a way for you to depend only on Him!

On this trip to Teleco, Milfort was with me and he had no money, as usual. When we attempted to get on the Tap Tap, I handed the driver all the money we had. Usually if it's a bunch of pennies, the driver would not bother to count them. On this particular day though, the driver stopped and counted out all the pennies! When he finished counting, it came up to only fourteen cents. I thought he would let us get on, but he said "No!" and was upset because he thought we were trying to cheat him. I pleaded with him, and so did Milfort, but without success. He refused to let us ride. We were about five miles from Cite Soleil, and it was a hot day in July. The temperature had to be over 100 degrees and violence was all around. We had no choice but to walk on that hot day, and why? Because we were one penny short. Since that day I have learned that pennies do count, that pennies are as important as dollars. Today when I'm getting my car washed or at a store, a gas station or even riding my bike, and I see a penny, I stop and pick it up. Sometimes people look at me funny, but it does not matter because I will never forget that day in Port-au-Prince when one penny caused me to walk five miles.

After about five weeks, Milfort left to solicit support for his clinic work from churches around Haiti and in the United States. I was left alone with Milfort's children and mother who helped me learn about the Haitian people, Creole and just how to survive in such a place. Soon after Milfort left, we all moved to St. Michel de L`Attalaye, the second largest city in Haiti. I was taken there by Milfort's cousin, a young girl named Cecilia. She was 15 years old. St. Michel de L`Attalaye is located in the mountains of Haiti, but is made up of a city portion, which is St. Michel, and a rural part, which is L`Attalaye. We would be living in L'Attalaye, and as hard as it was for me to believe, the poverty was even worse in L`Attalaye than in Cite Soleil. There were few cars, many of the people had very little clothing, and everyone looked malnourished. I didn't think it could get worse, but it did. Soon after I arrived I sat on the porch of the "house" we would be living in, looked around at the people and the poverty and just hated it all. It was hard to believe it could be worse in the mountains!

6:

“Labou” – The Mud

St. Michel de L’Attalaye has a population of about 700,000. In the countryside, in L`Attalaye, there is no electricity or inside running water. The houses in town, in St. Michel, are more developed. These homes are made of stone or bricks. They have windows and doors. Most of the homes in the countryside, in L’Attalaye, are made out of sticks covered in mud that gets hard in the sun, with roofs made of straw. Most of the people in L`Attalaye are farmers. They grow corn, beans, and tomatoes. There are also many fruit trees such as mango, banana, plantain, grapefruit, orange, and pineapple.

St. Michel de L’Attalaye is about 50 miles northwest of Port-au-Prince. It is only 50 miles away, but it takes 6-8 hours to reach Port-au-Prince because the roads are so bad. The nearest, largest city to St. Michel de L`Attalaye is Gonaives. It is 25 miles away and takes only an hour and a half to get there.

St. Michel sits on top of the one the largest mountains. The roads are not paved. Instead, the roads are made of rocks with ditches and holes. From the neighboring town of Ennery, where free Haiti’s founding father Toussaint L`Ouverture was born, to St. Michel, 13 rivers must be crossed. There are no bridges. The only choice is to drive through the rivers. The rivers are not dangerous except when it rains when they rise and become rapid. Many people have drowned in the rivers because of rain. People, cows and even homes have been washed away.

St. Michel is very dusty and rocky except during the rainy season of March-June. During the rainy season the rocky roads turn to thick, black mud. The mud is so thick it is like tar and smells from all the animals that walk the road on their way to the local market. This is how St. Michel de L'Attalaye got its nickname "Labou." Labou means mud in Creole. Trucks and cars going north get stuck in this mud. Sometimes it takes days to get them out. Sometimes people steal parts of the vehicles as they sit stuck in the mud. Not surprisingly, many people avoid St. Michel during this time of year.

Only a few people spoke a little of very bad English. All spoke Creole. There were only a few cars in L'Attalaye. There were lots of trucks for transporting fruit and charcoal to Port-au-Prince. Many people had bicycles, mostly ridden by the men. Some had donkeys and mules to help carry items to the market to sell, but most people walked. During the rainy season, not only would cars and trucks get stuck in the mud, but walkers too found the roads challenging.

Every Tuesday the women went down to the river to wash their clothes, take a bath, and wash their hair. It was a day for the women to get together and talk about current events. One Tuesday during the rainy season, I had to go to the river to wash my clothes. I had my clothes in a large wash basin, and started out toward the river. I had my sandals on, even though I noticed that no else did. I didn't understand how they could walk into that thick, smelly mud with no shoes! I stood and thought to myself: "I am not going into that mess with no shoes on." But as I stood there, children and women ran on ahead, splashing mud on me as they went. Too stubborn and proud, I kept standing. The nurse in me kept saying: "If you put your foot in there, something is going to get in your skin and make you sick!" So there I stood, needing to go forward to wash, but refusing to move. Finally the Lord said to me: "Dollie, you're going to have to go through the mud to get to the river. Once you're there, you can wash." I hesitated, but started to walk, keeping my shoes on. Of course, they immediately got covered in mud. In fact, they got stuck in the mud. Now not only did I have to take my feet out of my muddy sandals, but I had to reach down in the labou, this thick, tarry, sticky, smelly mud to get my sandals off. To my surprise, once I got my sandals off, it wasn't bad. I finally got to the river, washed myself and my clothes, and headed back. I got stuck in the mud again, but God kindly told me: "You're almost home. Walk in it and on the other side is home. You can wash again there."

That day I learned a valuable lesson. Life can be hot, stiff, tough, and smelly like the labou in L'Attalaye, and I may have to walk some muddy roads, and I may have to experience things I would like to avoid. I shouldn't be discouraged though, because ahead there is a river and I can wash myself there. God will always bring me out of the mud. I only have to trust Him to make the muddy way clear.

There were two open market days in St. Michel de L'Attalaye. The women would get up early and walk to the market. These market days were days of excitement, for then the women would be able to sit and talk to each other about all the events that had happened since the last time they met. To an outsider, the open market looked like an unorganized group of women sitting on the ground with baskets of items to sell. Once you learned the market, though, you understood that there was area for vegetables and an area for meat, bread, eggs, charcoal, clothes, and household goods. Market day was an all-day affair. It lasted from early in the morning to 6 pm. There were a couple of stores that had a generator, so they had ice and cold soda. They also had butter, canned milk, and candy. It was a joy to walk to town on market day, just to get a cold drink.

This open market in St. Michel is typical. Despite the unrelenting heat and seeming chaos, everything can be found at the market.

The people in St. Michel were not as friendly as the people in L'Attalaye. I was always greeted with "Bon Jour" ("Good Morning" or "Good Day" in Creole), in the countryside, but in town, people just stared. In time, this would change.

I lived in St. Michel de L'Attalaye 10 months out of the year for 13 years. For the two months when I went back to the United States, to Detroit, I visited my children and family. My church remained standoffish, but after articles about me and my work at the clinic appeared in the local newspapers and in the November 1988 issue of *Ebony* magazine, I got donations of money and medical supplies which I happily took back with me to L`Attalaye.

L`Attalaye, this dirty, poor village that I wanted to leave as soon as I saw it, was where I was taught about the Haitian people, their culture, religion, language and customs. The women and children of L'Attalaye taught me everything. It was also while I was living here that I fell in love with and married Milfort. During these years God truly proved Himself to me and showed me that He was my Protector, Provider, Encourager, Healer, and Friend. It was here where I really learned to pray and talk to God and to trust Him.

Many times when things got difficult and I felt alone, I would ask God why. Many times He would say nothing. But He did answer me. Once I was riding a bus which was overcrowded as usual, and I was having stomach pain. I sat on this hot and crowded bus, tired and miserable, unable to communicate with anyone because I hadn't yet learned Creole. I was crying and asking God "Why me? Why send me here, to St. Michel?" He softly spoke into my ear: "Remember the song you would always sing? 'Wherever you lead me I will follow?'" I did remember the song! I stopped crying. I had the sense that He was there. Another time I was again feeling very alone and went for a walk in a wooded area. I felt as if even my own family had abandoned me. Again I started to cry and asked God the same question, "Why me?" He again answered in a soft voice and asked me "Am I not enough?" I felt His presence again and thought, "He is with me! Of course He is enough." So St. Michel de L'Attalaye became my home. It is where I was transformed.

7:
The House in L'Attalaye

The house in L'Attalaye, where I would spend many years, belonged to Milfort. Cecilia, Milfort's 15 year old niece was the one he sent to Cite Soleil to pick me up. Cecilia picked me up and we got on a bus to begin to make our way to L'Attalaye. The hot and crowded bus took us as far as Gonaives where we transferred to a flatbed pickup which took us the rest of the way to L'Attalaye. Cecilia spoke no English and I spoke no Creole. Cecilia was a beautiful girl with thick, long black hair which she wore in two long braids. She also had a beautiful smile. Cecilia was my translator, my helper, my companion. She worked with me every day, teaching me how to buy medicine in Port-au-Prince and how to maneuver Haiti.

When we arrived in St. Michel, we were so dusty from being on the truck that all you could see of us were our eyes. We then had to walk four miles to L'Attalaye. I thought St. Michel looked bad with its unpaved roads and inconsistently built houses, but when we arrived in L'Attalaye, I was unprepared for what I saw. I saw straw roofs and leaf roofs, donkeys, mules, goats, and chickens running loose. I felt as if I had stepped back into the 19th century. Here I was, an RN, an educated, intelligent woman standing in the middle of nowhere, lost in time! Naked children were running and playing. People were just standing in their yards looked malnourished. What clothes they had on were ragged and needed washing, but they all smiled at me and said “Bon Jour, Miss!”

Many of my neighbors would gather outside my home in the evenings to spend time together. These girls do each other’s hair. There are no mirrors, so they have to trust one another to look their best.

Cecilia took me to the house. There was only one twin bed with a mattress, but no sheets or covering. Cecilia slept on the floor and I had the bed. There was no other furniture in the house except for one table and two chairs. There weren’t even pots or pans. There was an indoor bathroom just off the kitchen, but there was no running water, so neither the toilet nor the shower worked. The floor was cement and needed sweeping.

This house was the nicest one around. It was the only brick house and it had five rooms, doors and a tin roof.

The yard was unkempt. It was just some bricks on the ground, and some tropical green flowers in front. There were no screens on any windows or doors and it was very hot because of the tin roof. At night mice looked down at me from the wood ceiling above. I was afraid these mice would bite me, but they never did. I eventually lost my fear of the mice after much prayer to remove the fear because I knew the mice weren't going anywhere. And so began my journey in this house. It was here that sick people came to me and I did whatever I could to help. I couldn't yet speak Creole, but as they talked and pointed, and with Cecilia's constant help, I began to learn. Children and babies with their parents came in daily and I gave them what little medicine I had.

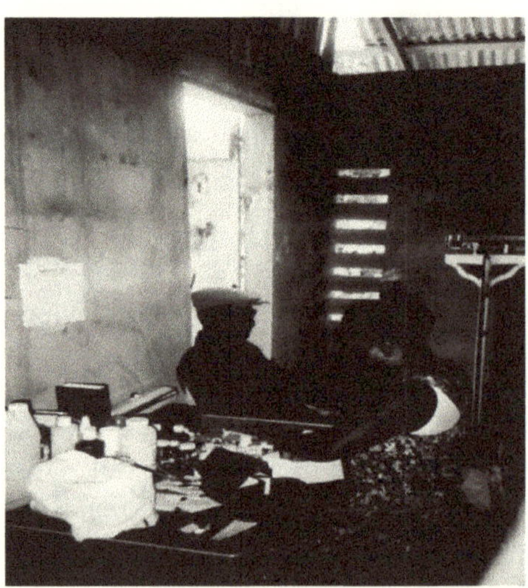

Here I'm seeing a curious witchdoctor at the clinic in L'Attalaye. He was treated for a sore on his hand.

It was in this house in L'Attalaye that I learned too how to depend on God. For instance, once, when my money ran out, I had to depend on God to help me. My canned goods were gone and I had no money to send Cecilia to the market. I had absolutely nothing to eat. I refused to eat the corn that the people ate. They roasted the corn until it was black. I said to myself that I would never eat such a thing. Besides, the people were so dirty! I didn't know it then, but I really had a problem. I needed God's molding, so God began His work. I prayed to God for a miracle, that He would send someone to L'Attalaye with enough food to feed me like He did the prophet Elijah, but He didn't send anyone with money or food. For several days I went hungry and still I refused to eat what they had. Finally, I came to myself and thought: "Why should I sit here and die when there is corn?" I got off my knees and told Cecilia to ask a little girl to bring me some of the corn. I boiled river water to drink. The girl came. She had no clothes and her hands were black with dirt. I was so hungry I didn't care how she looked. I ate that corn and drank the clean but nasty tasting river water, and I was filled and much satisfied. This was just one of my many humbling experiences in L'Attalaye.

The people of L'Attalaye taught me how to build a fire, and how to cook my food. When I had no matches, they taught me to get "a piece of fire" from someone else who had a fire going. As little as they had, they even gave me sheets for the bed. The house was just three minutes down the road from the clinic, and so became a place people in the village would gather. In the evenings people came to the house to talk and laugh with me even though I could not understand Creole. They couldn't pronounce Dollie, so they called me "Miss La." They helped me learn Creole by pointing and naming objects. Early on I thought I had learned how to say "Good Morning," but I kept saying "Jour Bon" instead of saying "Bon Jour" and the children really laughed at that. But they kept helping me and finally, with much prayer and their help, I did learn Creole.

I took whatever transportation was nearest at hand. I often rode a horse, a donkey, or a bicycle. My ability to ride a bicycle was surprising to many.

These boys are playing a board game in the evening after the day's work is done and the heat has abated somewhat.

Cecilia was my most important helper. She helped me in the house and also with going to the market in the morning. But even she had others to consider besides myself and herself. I didn't know for a long time that when she cooked a chicken for me, I only got a few little pieces because she was also feeding her brother, cousins, and friends! She was great company for me. Years later Cecilia died of AIDS.

In the beginning, the house was empty, almost uninhabitable. As time progressed, though, it became home. Years later, when I married Milfort, we fixed up the house. Furniture was made for each room. We would choose the Mahogany trees, have them cut down and tell the furniture makers how we wanted them to build the furniture. They made me a kitchen with cabinets, closets in the bedrooms, two dressers, and doors for the four rooms. Eventually I brought in a stove with butane gas. We got plumbing for the bathroom and kitchen. Most of the time it didn't work, but when it did, it was really nice. We had windows with screens put in along with a screen door. I bought paint in town and painted all the rooms. All the rooms were painted with bright colors. Behind the house I planted ferns, flowers, and had a vegetable garden. Banana plants were in the yard along with trees visiting Canadian missionaries had given us. The house really began to look like a home. After working hard every day in the clinic, it was nice to home come to an oasis. There was still no electricity, but it was clean and cool – a real home.

Cecilia and me in front of my cheerful yellow house and growing Mahogany trees.

Occasionally people in the area used the house for bridal showers and wedding receptions. There weren't many weddings because most people couldn't afford a dress, suit, a gold wedding band, and food to feed guests. Most marriages were common law marriages, but they gathered at the house nonetheless. They enjoyed seeing how an American lived. God had blessed this place, not just for me, but for others. Not everyone was so accepting of my presence in the village though.

Once the witchdoctor came and put a one-armed black Voodoo doll in the yard to frighten me away. I just picked up the doll and threw it away. I remember the scripture "Greater is He that is in you, than He that is in the world." I always told the people that God is greater than any devil or demon. Voodoo and Christianity don't mix well, and I was a threat to the witchdoctor's business. Every day I saw sick people for no charge. I also had someone to pray for them, usually a deacon from one of the churches. There was a spiritual warfare between the two religions. I was taking the patients away from the witchdoctor. I was taking his source of money, for the witchdoctors charged the people, and if one my patients accepted Jesus Christ along with getting better, it meant that the witchdoctor and other Voodoo believers lost a whole family to Christianity.

Another time the witchdoctor soaked a string in some kind of solution and hung it on the gate that led to my house. I was told that if someone touched the string, they would get sick or even die. Well, I thought, God is greater than the devil. I simply took the string off the gate and threw it in the road. People watched me remove the string and looked shocked when I did not get sick and fall down dead. The witchdoctor tried again. This time a group of people played their drums, chanted, and threw objects on the roof to scare me, but it didn't work. Then there appeared an open bowl with a cut off chicken head and corn in it along with a scribbled note, and several dark brown pennies in front of my gate. I just swept all of it into the road. Again people were shocked that nothing happened to me. The witchdoctor was trying his best to send me away. Most of his customers were now coming to me and getting better, and I wasn't charging them anything! In spite of all these attempts to get rid of me, the house and I stayed for years. God really watched over me and protected me!

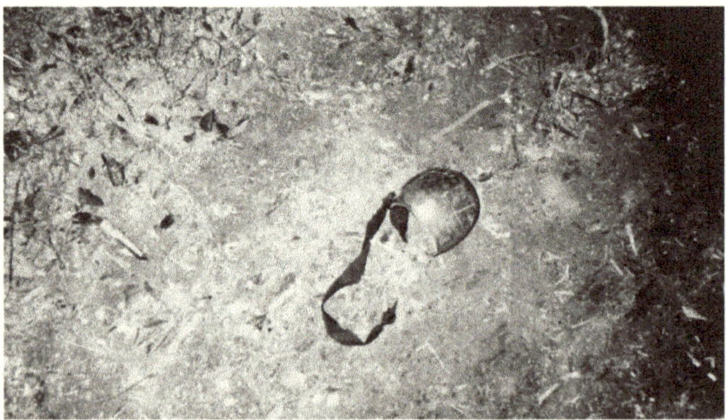

An example of Voodoo that I found on my front walk, intended to frighten me. This is a large, hollowed out fruit rind filled with corn, pennies, and a chicken head. The blue scarf indicates service to a loa.

8:
Cork

Cork was a four-year-old boy who came from a faithful Voodoo family. He and his family lived on the other side of the river from the house, toward St. Michel. Like most Haitian boys his age, Cork was small and underweight because he was malnourished. In the countryside it was the chore of small boys to water the cows and donkeys at the end of the day. If the family had pigs as well, they were included in the trip to the river to drink. One day, Cork was taking his cow to the river to get some water. He had one end of a rope around the cow's neck and the other end tied to his waist. Cork didn't realize how thirsty the large cow was, and so when the cow got closer to the river, it began to run down the hill to get to the water. Cork tried to keep up, but the cow was too fast. It dragged Cork down the hill. By the time anyone noticed, Cork was lying at the bottom of the hill, unconscious and bleeding badly from several cuts on his head.

I had been working in the clinic all day and was almost finished when I heard screaming and yelling from a large crowd of people running toward the clinic. They all had their Voodoo clothing on, the women in red head scarves and blue and red dresses. I thought they were going to a service, but they came into the yard. A man was holding something bundled up in a towel. The man, Cork's father, was screaming that if his son died, he wanted to die too, that he was going to kill himself. The mother was in a state of hysteria. When I unwrapped the towel, I placed the still unconscious Cork on a table and saw that he had massive head injuries. Rocks were embedded in his scalp, and he was bleeding from his ears. Both of these are bad signs. I didn't know what to do. I had so little at the clinic except for basic medical supplies. The clinic had only the basics of aspirin, worm medication, sutures, some IV solution, and some blood pressure medication. Anything I got I used, and when I ran out I ran out. I didn't know what to do, so I prayed. I asked God to spare Cork's life not for my sake, but for his father's.

After washing Cork's wounds, I bandaged him and told his parents to take him home. Cork was still unconscious and getting cold. I thought he would die before they even got home. Later that evening, God told me to go to Cork's hut and pray for Cork, so I did. The next morning God woke me early and said "Go see Cork." On my way up the road, people asked me "Is Cork dead?" I said "No." By faith I believed he would be alive. The faster I walked down the road, the brighter the sun began to shine. The devil spoke in my ear and said "He's dead," but I refused to accept this and trusted God. By the time I crossed the river, the same one that Cork was dragged to, I could see a crowd gathering in the yard of Cork's home.

His family lived in a two-room hut made of clay, with sugar cane leaves for a roof. When I entered the home I saw that the floor was dusty and dry with just two chairs and a table. I could not see in the back room. I had to bend down to get into the back room, and what did I see? Cork sitting in his mother's lap! God had worked a miracle. Cork's face was swollen and his eyes were just slits, but he was awake! The devil wasn't done though. The devil said "He can't talk." I gave Cork some cereal and some of it got on his mouth and he said "Clean my mouth." He could talk, eat, feel, and walk. I praised God and thanked Him. I nearly ran with happiness all the way back home. As I returned home, they asked me if God (Bon Dieu) had healed Cork. I said Jesus had healed him. I was so happy to see God that had worked another miracle!

About two weeks later we were in church and in came a man, a woman in a white dress, and a little boy in a brown suit and shoes. It was Cork with his father and mother. Both of Cork's parents accepted Jesus and left Voodooism. They became Christians and later married. They said Jesus was stronger than any "Loa," because He had saved their son. Cork had fully healed. Years later I saw Cork as an adult. He showed me the scars on his head and thanked me for saving his life. I said "It was Jesus."

9:

The Clinic

The clinic I worked out of was started by Milfort. It was about a quarter mile down the road from the house. It was built with cement blocks and had two rooms. The room I worked out of had a desk, a chair, an examining table, a cabinet to store medicine and supplies, an adult and baby scale, and that was it. Although I did not have much furniture or equipment, I saw thousands of patients over the 12 years I worked there. Usually I had one Haitian woman to assist. I tried to train several women to be nursing assistants, but all were illiterate, but one, Rose Marie Dacinne proved very helpful. Rose Marie had a fourth grade education. I would sometimes see 200 people a day and Rose Marie was a great help. From birth to death, illness, disease, wounds, whatever came our way Rose Marie and I did our best to help.

People came not only from L'Attalaye and St. Michel, but also from other towns as far as 15 miles away. Word got around. When the people came they knew they would leave feeling better. I had medications that were not expired, the clinic was free, and it was run by a missionary that loved them regardless if they accepted Christ or not.

Although the clinic was simple, it sat in a yard surrounded by mango, orange, grapefruit, and avocado trees. For years my husband Milfort and I would plant vegetables such as tomatoes, onions, beans, and beets.

One year we planted peanuts and even made our own peanut butter to eat and sell! One year we grew cantaloupes and watermelons. The watermelons were a bad idea though because whatever the goats didn't eat the people picked before they were ripe. Of the hundred or so melons we planted we only got to eat about three! But it was fun to see them grow. The clinic was not well supplied, but it was beautiful. We made it that way so that the sick would have something beautiful to look at while they waited to be seen.

People usually arrived early each morning about 5am. Some came on donkeys or mules. Some had to be carried on home-made stretchers made of sticks and cloth. Others walked or rode bikes. Some came in trucks. Whatever means they had to get to the clinic, they came. Some were already dying, some were already lame. They were old and young. They were preachers, witchdoctors, lawyers, and farmers. They all came looking for a miracle or for some relief from their suffering. The clinic hours were 8 am – 1 pm Monday through Friday. After 1pm it was just too hot to stay open. What the clinic offered was hope, encouragement, even possibly a cure or health. Everyday prayer was offered to God. Then there was singing and a scripture reading. People were then offered Jesus. Usually no one was interested, but sometimes one or two would say yes. The clinic was in the middle of a strongly Voodoo area. It did not matter if they accepted Christ. Love was shown to them anyway, and I believe that this too made a difference in the clinic. I just worked around all of these issues, for I knew that God was greater than any “Loa.” The people who were Voodoo believed in loa or demons whom the people always had to please or else some evil would befall them. It was often difficult to convince them that God offered a better way.

The wait at the clinic could last 4-5 hours. I would not leave until everyone was seen.

The clinic also brought business and commerce to L’Attalaye. When people came early, they would often be hungry so the women in the area would start cooking and selling food in front of the clinic. The women would cook beans and potatoes. They would sell bread with peanut butter, cola and water as well. This was good for everyone because many times people would have to wait 4-5 hours to see me especially on days when 100 people were waiting to be seen.

Large pots of rice and beans were often on the menu for the one main meal a day during a clinic day.

Sometimes the sickest ones died in the yard or on the porch before I could get to them. If they lived long enough to make it inside, usually they would make it. So many babies died in my arms. I was just too late. There was nothing I could do. There were so many who were at the end stages of starvation. Their hair was red, their bellies were swollen, their eyes were bulging, and the only medicine I had to give them was some liquid Tylenol to help them sleep until death came to relieve them of their misery. Those with cuts, infected wounds, skin rashes, colds, allergies, high blood pressure and other diseases too many to name came to the clinic sick, but left with a hope of being cured.

Once, a local witchdoctor brought one of his clients to the clinic. The witchdoctor's client had come all the way from New York City so that he could treat her. Her complaint was a severe headache. When I took her blood pressure, it was very high. I gave her some medication and told her not to eat too much salt, or greasy foods. I told her to rest for several days and then return to the clinic. At the end of two weeks her blood pressure had come down to normal and her headaches were gone. I asked her if she would "accept Jesus in her heart." She turned to the witchdoctor to ask his permission. Of course he said no. I asked her why she came all the way to St. Michel. Why didn't she see someone in New York? She explained to me that this witchdoctor was very wise. She could not understand that it was not his wisdom that made her blood pressure decrease, but the medicine and a prayerful nurse! She left, never thanking me and praising her witchdoctor.

When several witchdoctors in L'Attalaye reported me to the Minister of Health from Gonaives, the clinic was in danger of being closed. The witchdoctors were upset with me because they were losing a lot of their customers, and therefore a lot of money. At my clinic the patients didn't have to pay. The patients left with American medicines and they got better. In Haiti, when you go to see a witchdoctor, you have to bring some sort of payment. You brought money, a chicken, a goat, land or even children. If you did not get well, you dare not complain for fear that the witchdoctor will put a curse on you or your family.

So the Minister of Health came to investigate me. He explained that there had been a complaint against me and my clinic. The complaint was that I was using syringes when giving pain injections and as a result I was spreading HIV/AIDS. I explained to him that was not true because I used the syringes only once and then disposed of them. I threw them in the outhouse toilet. No one would get to them there. Then the Minister wanted to know why I was not charging people. He thought that my medicine must not be good, otherwise I would be charging something. Many Haitians believe that if you give them something and you don't expect anything in return, then it must not be any good. I explained to him that I was a Medical Missionary Nurse, and I showed him my license as an RN. He said that that didn't matter to him. He insisted that I must charge something at the clinic if I wished to remain open. Finally I agreed and so I started asking the people to pay one dollar Haitian, about 20 cents American. Many didn't even have that of course, but I did state the price daily. People brought fruit, eggs, chicken, sugar, and even some brought money.

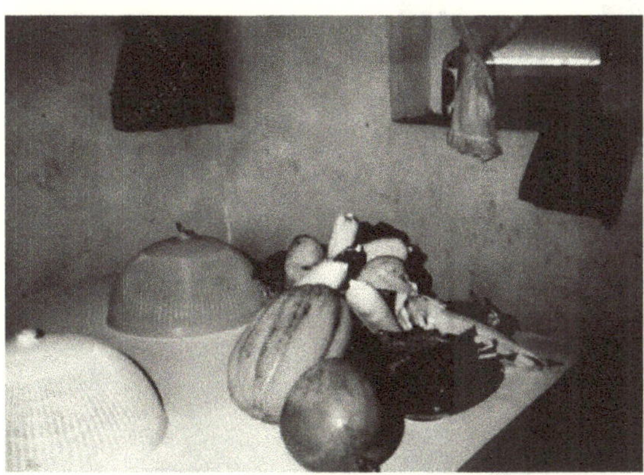

After increased pressure from local witchdoctors, I agreed to charge for the clinic visits. My patients often paid me with fresh produce.

The clinic was a light of hope in a very dark area. Even when there was no hope for a patient, I would pray and hold them, kiss them, and give them a little medicine to ease them. Some would go home and die, but they died with a hope for a better day and a bit of relief from the suffering.

I purchased the over-the-counter medications for the clinic from an agency in Michigan. Other prescription medications were given to me by doctors and nurses I knew. I was able to purchase some medicine in Port-Au-Prince when I ran out. During the embargo against Haiti in 1994, I ran out of medicine and had no money to buy any more. No planes were flying to Haiti, so nothing could be shipped there.

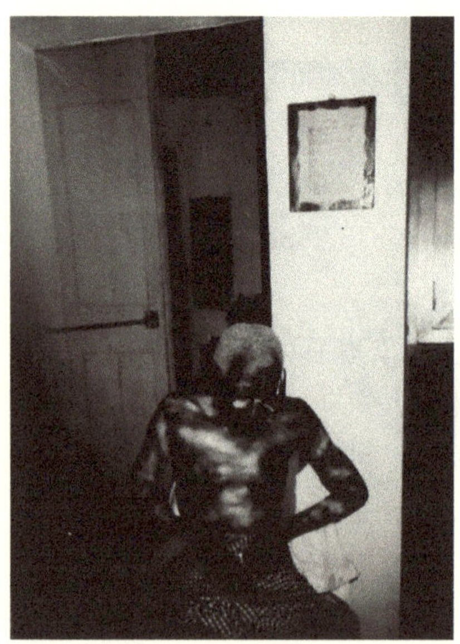

This man received rash treatment and a much needed pair of glasses at the clinic.

One day, of that same year, after the American military landed in Haiti, a group of Special Forces soldiers came to St. Michel. I did not know they were in town. A little boy ran into the clinic to tell me that some white American soldiers were in town and couldn't speak Creole. I walked as fast as I could into town and showed them my military ID card. At the time I was a captain in the U.S. Army Reserves Army Nurse Corps, and I out-ranked all six of the soldiers. They were very glad to see me and asked me what I was doing so far in the poor area. I explained that I was a Medical Missionary. We visited for about an hour, and then they gave me a ride back to L'Attalaye. Everyone along the way looked and pointed. I showed the soldiers the house and the clinic.

I had no medicine or supplies. My food was just about gone. One of the men gave me a case of MREs (Meals Ready to Eat). I was so grateful I didn't know what to say except "Thank you." The medic gave me some medicines and supplies. I believed God sent the men to St. Michel just for me. I gave them some bananas and peanuts. What they gave me was enough to last until the embargo was lifted and I could return to the U.S. and get more medicine. I will never forget that day. God again kept the clinic open.

Both the clinic and the house I lived in were on the main road from Saint Michel to L'Attalaye. Both were very visible and by living and working here both Milfort and I became public people. Many people were very curious about me as a foreigner. Foreigners rarely came to St. Michel. They were particularly fascinated with the fact that I was female and that I could ride a bike. Only men rode bikes in St. Michel, and no one had a car. Milfort and I spent a great deal of time together in the clinic. He taught me Creole and about Haitian culture. He asked me to marry him several times before I agreed. I had been so hurt by my first marriage I really had no interest in getting married again, but Milfort was persistent. After some time I realized that we shared the same ideas and the same goals. I finally said yes in 1988.

10:
TaTa

TaTa was a homeless, mentally disturbed man I met one day at the clinic. He looked like a typical homeless person, only worse. His clothes weren't just dirty, they were badly torn; half of his shirt was missing. He had no shoes and looked like he hadn't bathed in years. His teeth were yellow and greenish. His hair had not been combed in years. It was matted and I could see bugs in it. I could smell him before I saw him. He was also very friendly. He always had smile on his face and was constantly talking to himself. The people explained to me that TaTa was a Christian, but went to Voodoo services at night. He did this for a while. He was a Christian in the daytime and a Voodoo worshipper at night. As a result, some said, he lost his mind. Some others said he had a curse put on him, others said God was punishing him.

TaTa would start singing Christian songs and would end up singing Voodoo songs. He would run and leap and tear up whatever was in his way. The children teased and tormented him badly. They even threw rocks at him. Once they gave him a rotten chicken to eat. Because of his mental state, he started to eat it. I saw what was happening and intervened. I scolded the children and took TaTa under my care and supervision.

My husband and I thought we should begin by giving TaTa a bath and giving him some clothes. We put him in a large tin bathing tub. My husband scrubbed him a long time and washed his hair then cut it. We cut his toenails and fingernails. We gave him some of my husband's clothes. He looked like a different person.

TaTa wore those clothes until they almost fell off of him. Daily we fed him. He got used to being fed and would be at our gate around dinner time every day. TaTa began to gain weight, but he was still quite mentally ill. One day, after weeks of eating chicken (we usually ate chicken three or four times a week) he complained and said "Is that all you have? I've had enough of chicken!" And then he skipped, jumped, and tumbled down the road. It didn't take long for TaTa to get dirty. He was always tumbling and running into cacti and rolling in the dirt. Being dirty clearly did not bother him.

One Sunday morning the people of L'Attalaye came to me and said he was making too much noise. They asked if I could give TaTa some medicine to make him sleep. I did and he was asleep in about half an hour. When church was over, about three hours later, he was still sleeping. I was gripped with fear. I thought to myself "I have overdosed him and he will die and I will be arrested." My thoughts were really getting away from me. But after about six hours, he woke up, jumping, laughing and making his usual noise so I went into the house to get some dinner for him. We had rice, cabbage, beans, and chicken. He often ate in the clinic yard. Many people had started to gather to watch the two of us interact. As I watched him eat, many thoughts ran through my head. He was dirty again, from head to toe. He had lice in his hair and his teeth were again green and ragged. As I was thinking this, TaTa took the spoon he was eating with and offered to share the food with me! Immediately all of the nurse's information about infection and disease came to mind. I thought, "If I eat after him, I will surely get some deadly disease and die. My mouth and throat will be full of sores!" At that same moment, I looked at the people who were looking at me and TaTa, and I knew they were testing me. I remembered how I had been telling my patients that God is stronger than the devil and that nothing the devil does can harm you if you believe. So, with faith and trust in God, I opened my mouth and TaTa put the spoon he had been using into my mouth. I swallowed and said to myself, "Lord, in the morning, I know I will have sores." TaTa wasn't done. He then offered me a sip of the orange soda I had given him. He had already had some. When I looked at TaTa his teeth seemed even greener, and the rest of him seemed dirtier than ever. Then I saw the people of L'Attalaye watching. Their eyes got wide when I took a sip without wiping the bottle. They looked amazed. I guess they thought that I must surely drop dead, but I didn't. TaTa had accomplished a purpose: would she trust in God or the devil? I had no choice but to drink the cola. I must have really trusted God. I jumped up early the next morning and grabbed a broken mirror and looked. No sores, no sore throat, no fever! That night before I went to bed, I prayed that God would protect me and I believed God's word that "If you eat any deadly poison and you believe, it won't harm you."

Tata stayed around for several months, jumping, playing, lying on the road to sleep, but he never tested me again. I loved TaTa for his simple child-like trust. He never again wanted a bath or clean clothes. Every day I prayed for him and told him that I loved him and hugged him. He started calling me "Momma." A year after TaTa had moved on to some other village, I heard that he had his mind back and that he was attending church regularly. I thank God for allowing TaTa into my life. What he taught me was a truly humbling experience.

11:
Madame Idason

Madame Idason was one of the many women who taught me how to live and survive in St. Michel. She was married to a young pastor and had three small children ages 5, 6, and 7. Madame Idason was a tall, stately woman, about 30 years old. She lived with her family off of the main road about a half mile from Milfort and me in a two room hut. Her husband farmed and she helped, along with raising their three children. She could neither read nor write. She was a very quiet woman, and very strong and kind. She often sent me food when she cooked for her family. She always shared what she had, no matter how little. Both she and her husband were Christians. They had left Voodoo and were members of our church.

I had gone to Port-au-Prince for a short visit to check my mailbox to see if there was any news from home, and to see if anyone had sent me money. I would usually take this trip once a month. During one of these trips, Madame Idason was about 8 ½ months pregnant. I knew that she was expecting to deliver at any time. By the time I got back to St. Michel, about two weeks after I left, Madame Idason had died. When I heard this, I was shocked! The people said that Pastor Idason had called in three witchdoctors when Madame Idason's delivery became difficult. Apparently she was in labor for several days, but could not deliver. The women told me Madame Idason was screaming and in uncontrollable pain and then had a seizure. In his panic, her husband did what he would have done before he became a Christian. He had called on a witchdoctor once before when his wife was having difficulty in labor. This child had died, but Madame Idason had recovered. I did not understand why Pastor Idason called on three witchdoctors this time, having become a Christian. When I asked him, he said that he did this because of Madame Idason's family. Her family was not Christian; they were Voodoo believers. He told me that after seven days of his wife being very ill, she began to shake and tremble. On the eighth day Pastor Idason put his wife on a bed to carry her to town to see a medical doctor, but she died on the way. It was a needless death. If he had taken her to the doctor the first time she had a seizure, I knew that Madame Idason would still be alive. After she died, they took the baby, which of course had died as well. They said it was a large boy.

After Madame Idason died, the three witchdoctors who could not save her argued whether the baby and mother should be buried together in the same casket and grave. They buried both Madame Idason and her son in the same wooden coffin. I was so sad about Madame Idason's death. She was a Christian woman who died a horrible death, and now had to wake up in eternity to answer to God. I realized that it really means something to say that we are saved! Be saved! Stay saved! Jesus can fix it for you. If Jesus can't fix it, it can't be fixed. It is better to go to heaven in a sick body than to hell in a well body. It's really sad to go to hell in a sick, tormented body only to wake up in everlasting torment!

It would be many years before Pastor Idason would come back to Christ. For years he lived in shame. But thanks were finally due to God. Pastor Idason did, finally, come back to Christ.

12:
Son Son

He just had a headache on Friday evening, but by Saturday he could not talk. And then, Tuesday at noon he died. Son Son had died, and he died without Christ! That was the talk in St. Michel when they were preparing his body for burial. Son Son drank rum just about every day. He was a friendly man; he always spoke to people, but he was always drunk, staggering and unsteady down the road he went, often stumbling and falling down. He was 65-70 years old and had one daughter who lived in the United States. Son Son was raising his only grandchild, a three year old boy. Son Son would often come to the clinic with his grandson who usually had a cold or a skin rash – he always looked malnourished. Son Son would sit quietly and listen to me when I asked people waiting in the clinic if there was anyone who wanted to have Jesus come into their heart. Son Son would hear the gospel, listen to me and then say "Not now, later." Now later was too late.

Mary, the young lady who lived next door to me and did my cooking and washing, called me one Sunday afternoon and told me of Son Son's condition. I went to his one room hut built out of white washed dried mud and covered with dried hay and there Son Son lay. He was unable to speak and I knew right away that he had had a major stroke. There was nothing I could do but pray. I told his wife to notify his daughter because he may die. I went to see him the next evening.

Son Son was having small seizures and looking as if he were really fighting death. He still could not speak. I told his wife that Son Son's condition was worse. She began to cry. Tuesday morning Son Son's wife no longer asked me to help. Son Son had not died yet, but he lay so still both his wife and I knew death was over him. His eyes were open and staring. Later that day he did die. I went to help to prepare his body for burial.

Before the burial of the dead, the men prepare the body for the funeral which usually costs a family about $5. They tied a cord around Son Son's neck to keep blood from coming out of his mouth. They then took him outside the hut. There they bathed him with orange leaves and soap. This was done by one man. We took Son Son back into his hut. There we dried him off and put him in clean underwear and a white shirt. While we were bathing Son Son outside the hut the women had put the bed back in the hut and put a clean, pressed white sheet on it. We laid Son Son on the bed. I tied a string around his head and chin to close his mouth. They put a white sheet on him and another sheet in the doorway of the hut and a white curtain in the window. This let everyone passing by know that death had been there. Later they put three crosses in his bed. One at his feet after his toes were bound together, one on his belly button, and one under his pillow. Later they put half a bottle of rum in his hand. I was so sad knowing that Son Son wouldn't take another drink in this world or the next! After the body was ready the women began to wail and mourn for him. Tomorrow they would bury him, alone, by himself without Christ, in a Voodoo cemetery.

One day when I was on my way to my mother-in-law Charity's house in St. Michel, I heard three small children singing "Oh Oui La Mort"! What caught my attention was that they were singing with such passion. They were lying under a food shed with no clothes on. They were dirty, lying on a mat and singing themselves to sleep! They looked to be about 4 or 5 years old. What they were singing was "Oh, yes, death come! Oh, yes, death come!" Can you imagine? Death is so common that small children sing themselves to sleep with a death song. This song is usually sung when someone is dying and the people come to sit and wait on death. They all sing "Oh Oui La Mort." Most children this age in developed countries are singing "Mary Had a Little Lamb" or "Humpty Dumpty," not a song about asking death to come! Death is like a familiar person in Haiti. Every day people are dying and you can hear cries of death at several houses during the day and night. But to see these three small children singing "Oh Oui La Mort" over and over again until they were asleep was just so sad!

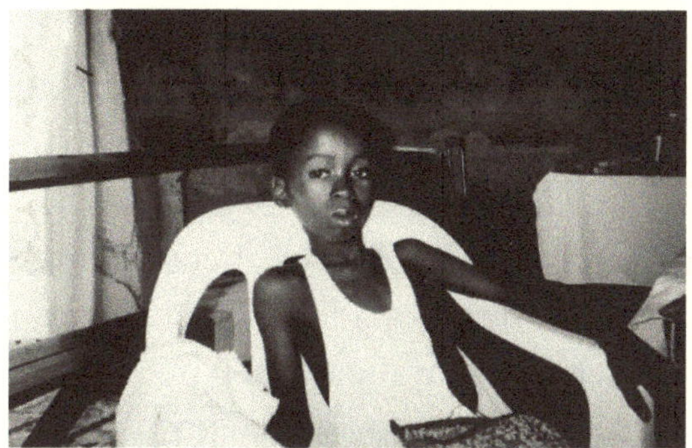

Samuel is 12 years old in this photo and malnourished. He survived because a donor was found who funded his visit to a hospital where he got the necessary IV. The clinic has no IV, and so typically malnourished patients do not survive.

These boys are happy to bring lunch to a relative.

13:
Witchdoctors

After I had lived in St. Michel for about 8 years, I heard the story about the death of a local witchdoctor who lived in St. Michel. Some of the women in L'Attalaye told me that the witchdoctor had people sitting in his yard for treatment as usual when he got sick. The people stayed in his yard for two days, waiting for the witchdoctor to heal himself. The witchdoctor died within 48 hours. The people didn't cry for his death because they were waiting for him to get back up! He died at 8am and the people waited until 6pm, and when they finally realized he wasn't going to get back up to help them, they cried. He was buried that night. The women who told me this story told me that some people came and stabbed the witchdoctor several times while he was in his coffin in the ground. Then another witchdoctor came to the grave to see if he was going to rise. When this witchdoctor realized that the body had been stabbed several times, the women told me the witchdoctor began to cut off parts of the body. The people said and believed that if you have the head of a witchdoctor, you can inherit his power! Sad!

TèSe was the highest witchdoctor in the area. I was told that he could sit in fire and not be burned. People said he had great power. People would come from all over Haiti and the United States for him to "treat" them or do some kind of magic or spells for them. TèSe lived on a compound with most of his children and grandchildren and their spouses. His wife was a mambo, a female witchdoctor. Her name was Madame TèSe and she was a very slender woman with a large smile that she flashed as often as she could. She had dentures which showed that they had money. But there was something about her eyes that looked dark to me. She later adopted me as her daughter.

Madame TèSe and her husband had been married about a year before. I remember the day of their wedding. It was a big event in L'Attalaye. They went to a Catholic Church in St. Raphael, a city about 10 miles south of L'Attalaye. They both rode on horses. To ride on a horse meant you had money or status which both of them had accumulated over the years. They had lived together for years, and had decided to finally marry. Madame TèSe had a full wedding dress and TèSe had on a suit and tie and shoes, and he gave his bride a ring. When they returned to their house, there was a big celebration. They whole community was invited. Their wedding and the celebration afterward was a large demonstration of wealth – something very few people had in St. Michel. They had chicken, goat, rice, and beans for everyone, and, of course, all the rum a person could drink. They had drum music and dancing until late in the night. They lived about a half a mile from my house.

Their compound was large with several houses. To enter their compound you had to step over "VeVe" writing. This is writing that is written on the ground with white powder. VeVe writings consist of symbols and letters. The purpose of this writing is to protect the people who live inside the compound from evil spirits (loas). There was also a large black crucifix about two feet high at the entrance to the house. It served the same purpose: for protection against evil spirits. Besides the many houses on the compound, there was a house of worship where TèSe performed his Voodoo services. Inside of this small building was an altar, a statue of Moses holding the Ten Commandments, a mambo doll, and a rum bottle decorated with bright jewels. Rum is used a lot in Voodoo services. It is used for healing and casting spells. There were also bottles that contained objects. There was a long whip that was often used in services. It is also used to beat the dead or zombies when witchdoctors get them out of the ground. The whip is used a lot in their services to conjure up their loas.

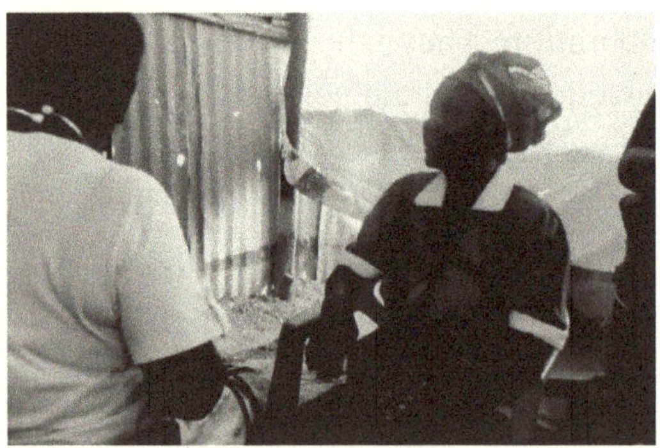

I treated this mambo for high blood pressure.

On his compound, TèSe also had chickens, goats, and donkeys. To the local people he was very wealthy. Both TèSe and his wife came to the clinic for physical ailments, like a skin rash or an infected cut. Sometimes I believe he came to get the medicine and used it to treat people when they came to him. He would also send his children when they got sick with a cold or fever. One of his teenage daughters got attached to me and liked being around me. She would come to my house and sit with me and sometimes comb my hair. Her name was Annette.

One summer Annette got pregnant. She was seventeen years old. She began to be very sick with fever, and TèSe sent for me. The person that came to me with the message from TèSe asked me to come, but also asked me not to let the people see that I was coming to see TèSe's daughter. So I put everything I needed in my pockets in my skirt. I took my stethoscope and medicines, and put it all in my pockets. When I arrived at the compound, there were three witchdoctors sitting outside the house in their traditional red shirts and red hats looking at me suspiciously. TèSe said he wanted me to come back in a day or two to see his daughter, but first he was sending for some strong "black water" to heal her. If it didn't work, he said, he would send for me again. This "black water" was from a certain river. It was said to have healing power. This is what TèSe used on his patients who came to him with fever.

The black water did not work so he sent for me again. When I entered the compound, after stepping over the VeVe and praying for Christ to help me, I spoke to the three witchdoctors who were still sitting outside the house where Annette was lying. I spoke very politely and respectfully to them. They bowed their heads. TèSe then took me inside and into a large room in his house. His home was made of bricks, was washed with white mud, and had a tin roof. It had several rooms. Many of his grandchildren were looking at me and a large crowd of people had gathered to see if Annette was going to be healed or if she was going to die. This was a custom of the people. In the middle of the large room lay Annette. She was lying on a bed. In her hair was a large black candle that had been partially melted, intertwined with her hair. She had multiple strings with colored beads tied around her pregnant stomach. There were burn marks on her abdomen, chest and arms. All these marks were the work of the witchdoctors to cast evil spirits out of Annette and to remove the curse they believed her boyfriend or his ex-girlfriend had put on her. TèSe and his family believed that this illness was a curse put on her by her boyfriend or his ex-girlfriend because she was jealous of Annette's pregnancy.

TèSe said he would give me three days to heal his daughter. Otherwise he was going to use those three witchdoctors sitting outside. This was a test to see if I had the power or if my medicine had the ability to heal his daughter. TèSe was not mean, but he stated it very frankly. He said he had spent a lot of money on this black water, but it hadn't worked and Annette was getting worse. Earlier that week I had been reading in the Bible about the prophet Elisha. God had told him it was going to rain. Elisha sent his servant to look for a sign. After going out looking for a sign several times, finally the servant said "I see a cloud the size of a man's hand." Elisha told his servant to get ready, it was going to rain. Little did I know I would need this scripture text to help me.

I asked Annette what the problem was. She said she was just sick. Although I could not pray out loud so as to respect TèSe and his family, I was praying all the time in my mind that Jesus would help me and show me what to do. I felt Annette's head and determined that she had a high fever. She was very hot and not perspiring at all. I asked for a tub to bathe her as a nurse not as a Christian missionary. I knew I had to cool her off quickly. All the while I was praying that Jesus would work a miracle. I kept bathing Annette with cool water and gave her Cipro 100 mg, an antibiotic. Her mother asked if she could put some herbs in the water. I said it was okay. Her mother asked if she could put some leaves in the water. I said okay again. I prayed and I bathed. I knew I couldn't say the name "Jesus" aloud, so I prayed silently, but nothing was happening. All the children and grandchildren were staring at me, and the three witchdoctors were all looking at me, this Christian nurse/missionary from the United States.

While TèSe was looking along with his friends, I prayed and asked God to show me a sign that the fever was broken. All of a sudden I saw three small round beads of sweat on Annette's nose. I began to praise God silently. Then the beads of sweat on her forehead started. I thought about the small cloud Elisha's servant saw. Elisha was God's prophet. I said "Lord, let it rain."

Annette began to sweat profusely, and she said she felt better. I left thanking God.

The next evening they sent for me again. They said Annette was sick again. I did the same procedure I did the day before. When I arrived I saw the same three witchdoctors sitting in the same place. This time Annette was lying on the bed again, but the candle was out of her hair and all the strings were gone. Again I bathed and prayed. Once again God caused the fever to be broken and she felt better, and again I left praising God.

The next day they sent for me again. Same thing: same witchdoctors, same people. This day was number three. If God didn't completely heal Annette, then the witchdoctor would have won. This time when I entered the house, Annette looked better and she was sitting on the side of the bed. I knew she was better because prayer changes things, along with Cipro 100mg over three days. I bathed and prayed and this time I told Annette that we were going to go outside after she began to sweat.

Annette's hair was a mess, all matted, dirty and flakes of the candle remained in her hair. Most women and girls don't care about how they look when they are sick, but the minute they start feeling better they want their hair combed. I asked God to give me a sign that He had healed Annette. When Annette came outside the house everyone was startled. She was holding onto my arm. I told her that Jesus had healed her and she was much better, but she had to believe. We walked around the house one time and then she sat in a chair. She reached up and patted her matted, dirty hair and said "My hair needs combing!" Everyone laughed. God had done it again. From that day on she got stronger and stronger. A few months later, contrary to what the witchdoctors thought, Annette gave birth to a healthy baby boy, no problems at all.

My prayer and hope is that even though TèSe's family are Voodoo worshippers, the grandchildren will remember the day a missionary came to help their aunt and sister and she got well. Jesus is stronger than any power. Maybe one day they will turn and worship God and become Christians.

Patients waiting for treatment at the clinic . The woman in the front is a local mambo.

Haiti's first democratically elected president Jean-Bertrand Aristide was a former Catholic priest whose mother was Voodoo. Aristide saw the importance Voodoo held for the Haitian people and was ex-communicated because he welcomed Voodoo, thought it should be recognized as an official religion of Haiti. He even allowed it in the constitution of Haiti. Aristide was ex-communicated for his beliefs. Catholicism and Voodoo had a ways to go before they lived together in harmony.

14:

Anne Marie

It was on a Sunday afternoon and I felt like something was not right with Anne Marie. Anne Marie was a neighbor, a friend, a mother and a wife. She lived across the road from me in L'Attalaye. Anne Marie lived with her common law husband, Frank, who was the oldest son of Madame Frank and her husband, Frank, another known alcoholic in town. The entire family was Voodoo worshippers. The lived on a compound like TèSe – several small huts with different family members living in each hut with one open kitchen. Unlike TèSe, though, they were very poor. The small children often ran around without any clothes on and they only cooked one meal a day.

Madame Frank suffered from severe asthma attacks. She had several children, mostly teenagers and one younger girl. They were very fond of me. We were very close. This family would come to the clinic for care for their colds, infections, and other mostly minor reasons. Anne Marie's parents were also both Voodoo worshippers. Her father had the title of "Guardian of the Dead." It was his job to assist the local witch doctor when it came time to get "dead people" from the grave.

I met Anne Marie when she came to the clinic. She had a terrible cough. As I listened to her lungs they had a diminished sound. She also had a bad skin rash and she only weighed about 90 pounds. She was very weak. It was my conclusion that she either had tuberculosis or was HIV positive. I prayed for her and gave her some Bactrim medication along with some cough medicine and medication for sleep. She began to get better. As long as I had some Bactrim or Cipro medication to give her, she was able to function, but if the medication ran out, she would get worse again. Anne Marie was my friend; we would often sit together and talk. We talked about her life, about living with both parents in Voodoo and her struggle living with her mother-in-law who did not like her. Anne Marie had three small children, ages 4-7. She could not read or write, and she did not know how old she was, which was common in L'Attalaye. She was not allowed to leave the compound except to come to the clinic or to go to the market in St. Michel. Many times when I would enter the clinic, I would see Anne Marie across the street at her compound. I would smile, wave and ask her how she was doing.

About a year after we met, Anne Marie got very sick. Her husband came to me and told me he had tried healing her. Frank was also a small-time witchdoctor. He wanted me to come and see Anne Marie to see if I could help her. I went to the small hut where she lived. She was lying on the one bed in the hut. She had lost more weight. She could not take care of herself or her family. I asked her if she would like prayer and if she would like accept Jesus. At first she hesitated and did not say anything. She looked puzzled. I told her I could give her some medicine, but that she needed Jesus. She then asked Frank if she could convert – she never said Jesus' name. Frank told her that he did not have any money to buy her a white dress, the color converts often wear, nor did he have any money to buy a rooster. Roosters were used as a sacrifice the people would offer to their loas. Frank said she should ask her loas for permission to convert. Anne Marie again looked puzzled. Then she said yes. Frank told her "You are just doing that to please Miss La." Anne Marie then got down on her knees and bowed her head. I told her to say the name of Jesus and that He would forgive her of all her sins. She could not say His name at first. Then as I prayed for her, I rubbed her throat, and then she uttered "Jesus" and tears began to fall down her cheeks.

Anne Marie accepted Jesus and became a Christian. She had never been in a church, had never read the Bible, but Jesus met her down in that dirty hut, way down in L'Attalaye! Anne Marie jumped up with a new lease on life. She had a red scarf on her head, which Voodoo worshippers wear, and she ran into the other room, found a white scarf and put it on her head. She got a broom and began to sweep the dirt floor. Her three children began to smile. Even Frank was smiling. They had a skinny, matted dog and even he looked happy. Everyone in the house was glad.

It was after becoming a Christian that she made me promise her that when she died, I would not let her family give her a Voodoo funeral or put things into or on her body when she died. Anne Marie realized that she would not live long, but she knew she would be going to a better place. She was not afraid. She had peace of mind and joy. So I promised Anne Marie I would see to it that she was treated like a Christian.

Anne Marie never did go to church. Frank would not allow it, and he was still a witch doctor, but she had church inside her. Daily I would see her in the yard sweeping, cooking, and singing church songs. For a while she was better. One day, though, I did not see Anne Marie in the yard and I had a feeling. I walked to her little hut and asked the family where she was. Madame Frank said that Anne Marie was in the house lying down. When I went inside, I was shocked by what I saw. There lying on the dirt floor (usually when a family thinks you are near death, they take you out of bed and lay you on the dirt floor), Anne Marie lay looking like she weighed about 50 pounds. She was almost unconscious and covered with ants. There were ants even coming out of her nose and ears! I was outraged! How could a human being allow someone to lay there and die like this? Immediately I picked her up in my arms and carried her to her bed, all the while blowing ants out of her nose ears and mouth. She whispered softly to me and said "Please don't leave me. Watch over me."

I bathed her and put some clean clothes on her even though her family thought it a waste since she was dying. It was hard to explain to them that a person can die with dignity. I sat at the foot of her bed so she could see me. Her mother-in-law sat at the head of her bed. Madame Frank said I was wasting my time siting with Anne Marie, but I knew I had to keep my promise. I sent for her mother and father, but the message came back that they were not coming because they had to do work for their loa and besides, Anne Marie had left her loa to become a Christian.

Anne Marie slipped into a coma about 9 pm. When the people heard she was dying, they began to gather and drink rum, play dominoes, and wait for her to die. This is the custom of the poor Haitian people in the rural areas of Haiti. Later that night, Anne Marie began to take her last breaths. By this time the people had sent for a wooden coffin, a new dress, stockings, panties, and a bra. All of this had to be put on her after she died. She began to gargle a little, so I repositioned her. Her mother-in-law told me again that that was unnecessary because Anne Marie was going to die anyway. I was only trying to make Anne Marie a little more comfortable, so I didn't listen to Madame Frank.

Anne Marie died at midnight. As I promised, I stood watch over her. I helped the "burial of the dead." These are the men who wash and dress the body after death. A hole was dug and lined with large leaves. After bathing Anne Marie, we brought her back into the hut. By this time a white curtain was hung in the doorway, letting everyone know that she had died. People were screaming and rolling around on the ground with grief. I could hear people crying and screaming from what seemed like miles away. The men started to put a penny in her mouth and I told them not to do it. Voodoo believers put coins in the mouths of the dead so that the dead can have some money when they get to the other side. After putting her clothes on, the men wanted to tie her hands and put a cross in them. I said no again – the cross was for protection from spirits of the other world.

Next they wanted to sprinkle dirt on her body. I said no once again. They respected me and did as I asked.

After the family had viewed her body, I placed some flowers inside Anne Marie's coffin. Bright orange poppies grew everywhere in L'Attalaye. Someone had given me poppy seeds years before and I planted them in my yard. When I came to live in L'Attalaye, there were no flowers. It was so dry that when I planted the poppy seeds the wind blew them and then they grew everywhere!

It came time for Anne Marie to be buried. I stayed with her until they nailed the coffin shut. No Voodoo rituals had been done to her body. She was a Christian and I made sure that I kept my promise. Anne Marie was carried from her yard through a cut out piece of the cactus fence. They never carry the dead person out through the gate because they don't want death to enter again, so they take the body through a new part of the fence. Anne Marie was taken to a Voodoo cemetery and buried. Although Anne Marie's body was buried in a Voodoo cemetery, her soul was with Jesus. One day I will see her again, my Anne Marie.

15:
Yolean

Yolean was about an 18 year old girl. She had lived in L'Attalaye, but had left to go to Port-au-Prince to get a job when she was about 17. While she was in Port-au-Prince she got sick. Some thought it was hepatitis or AIDS. When she returned to L'Attalaye she was very sick. She was very weak and had lost about 15 pounds, which put her at about 90 pounds. Her skin had a yellowish tone to it and her eyes were yellow, which led me to believe she had Hepatitis.

Yolean came to the clinic and I treated her for the high fever she had, and gave her some vitamins and pain medication. After about a week she got better. She started to gain some weight and was able to get up and walk around.

There were days when Yolean would come sit with me after I was finished working in the clinic. She was learning to speak English and she was helping me to learn more Creole. She would point to an object and say it in Creole and then I would say it in English. Sometimes we would both laugh because we could not pronounce the words correctly. She could not pronounce the English words clearly and I could not roll my tongue to pronounce Creole words. Sometimes she would stay and eat dinner with me. Sometimes she would teach me the Haitian church songs. We would sing for hours. Sometimes she would help me wash my hair and comb it for me. Oh, what a time we had together, laughing, talking and just being silly!

Yolean lived with her mother and younger sister. They lived in a small one-room hut off the main road in the woods in back of my house. It was very dusty and had lots of bushes. Her father was a very intermittent presence in her life – a typical father-child relationship in many families, but she was well-loved by her mother. As the great hope for the family, it was hoped that Yolean would go to Port-au-Prince, find work and send money back home to L'Attalaye to help support her mother and sister. Yolean's mother worked a small strip of land growing different kinds of vegetables which she would then sell in the market. Yolean's mother was also a Voodoo worshipper. As a Voodoo worshiper, Yolean's mother believed in Bon Dieu, the good god. Bon Dieu watched over the Voodoo worshippers with help from the loas or demons as we Christians call them. Yolean, however, was a Christian. I never found out how Yolean became a Christian. When I met her she had already been baptized and took Communion in church every month.

I really enjoyed talking to Yolean every day. I learned that she had a boyfriend in the city, and that she thought that he somehow had made her sick. She never discussed with me whether she was sexually active, but I believed that she was and that she was HIV positive from him.

HIV/AIDS is very prevalent in Haiti. Many of the boys/men don't like using condoms. Once, the Health Department in Detroit gave me over 300 condoms to distribute in Haiti. One day at the clinic I gave every man five or six condoms and asked if they knew how to put them on. They all said yes. The next day when I got to the clinic, I saw all the children in front of my house with these clear "balloons." The children were filling them up with water or air and throwing them up into the air! There were "balloons" everywhere!

I had hoped that Yolean would get better, but I knew that she would not. She kept losing weight and had started to get a rash on her chest and back, both signs of AIDS. She also began to cough a lot and when I listened to her lungs, her breath sounds were diminished which meant her lungs were infected. Her mother could not afford to put her in the hospital, and I knew it was just a matter of time before Yolean got worse. After a few months, Yolean began to lose more weight and her jaundice increased. She lost her appetite and was lying in her bed. She was a skeleton – no fat at all. Her eyes were bulging, her teeth protruding because even her lips had no fat. I could count every rib. She had a scarf on her head, but when I took it off I saw that all her hair had fallen out. She was no longer the pretty lively girl of just a few months earlier.

One day when I was sitting on my porch, I noticed that some people were carrying someone on a homemade stretcher to the witchdoctor. Then I saw Yolean's father whose mother was a witchdoctor, and I knew that he was taking Yolean to his mother.

Later that week I went to see Yolean at her grandmother's about a half mile away, and she begged me to take her from her grandmother's house. She said that they had been doing all sorts of magic on her to get her better. Yolean said that she was still a Christian and that she did not want to stay there. I asked her father's permission to take Yolean home with me and he said that was all right.

As time went on, Yolean's condition did not improve. I took care of her the best I knew how. I fed her with a spoon, bathed her, and gave her medicine to make her feel better. I would rub her with oil and lotion. I would hold her in my arms and pray with her and sing songs to her. I prayed and prayed that God would heal her, but things did not change. In fact, they got worse. Yolean dropped to about 60 pounds. I could lift her and carry her about the house without feeling tired. During this time we got even closer. Her mother would come and sit for a while, but not long because she had to work in her garden. Her sister would come by and visit, but her father and grandmother would not come. Many times it was just Yolean and me. I hurried home to her when I finished working in the clinic. She started to get a bit better.

Yolean did not have clothes to fit her. She wanted to have underwear that would stay on her body. I did not have any that would fit her so I asked her mother if she could buy Yolean a couple pairs of panties. I would have bought them myself if I had the money. No one had money. I asked Yolean's father if he could. I knew he could get the money if he didn't have it. His response to me was that he was saving money to buy her a coffin and to feed the people after she died. When he said this I was so angry and shocked. I didn't know what to do. I could not tell Yolean, so I put a pair of my large underwear on her.

Then Yolean's condition worsened to the point that I called her father to take her back to her mother. I told Yolean that I would not leave her and would be there for her. She cried and they took her away. Every afternoon when I finished my work at the clinic, I went to be with Yolean. She was in and out of consciousness, but she knew I was there. Once she cried out "The loa is here to get me!" I held her in my arms and assured her that no evil spirit was going to get her. She then relaxed. The people were beginning to gather around the house, waiting for her death. The men had put up the table for dominoes and began to play. They got the white curtain ready and the rum. They were all waiting for Yolean to die.

Later that evening I was still siting with Yolean. I got up and went to get some church people so that they could sing and pray for Yolean. They read the 27th Psalm to her and sang "The Lord be with you, He will never leave you." All of Yolean's family members were Voodoo worshippers. I held her in my arms as she lay dying. She opened her eyes to me and said "Miss La, I'm going home. Will you look for me when you get there?" I replied with tears in my eyes "Yes, I will find you."

Yolean never said another word to me or to anyone else. I looked for her mother so that she could be with Yolean until she died, but I could not find her. Someone else did find her though and she came to her daughter. At first Yolean's mother did not want to hold Yolean, so I kept holding her, with tears in my eyes and my heart full of hurt.

Yolean was lying on the dirt floor in the fetal position. Someone came from the back of the house and tried to straighten her arms and legs. This they did to prepare them for death. I got angry, and told them to leave her alone, for when she died her limbs would relax. The people knew how fond I was of Yolean, so they left her alone.

Yolean's mother finally agreed to hold her, but she really did not want to because she said she could not stand to see her daughter die. It was the custom that if a child was dying, the mother would hold that child until it died. I explained to Yolean's mother that she was there at Yolean's birth and so she needed to be there at her death.

The church sang songs to Yolean and they read the 27th Psalm, and when they got to the verse "When thou father and mother forsake thee, then I will take thee up," a tear rolled down Yolean's face and she took her last breath and died.

As usual, after Yolean died, the people began to show their emotions. They were hollering, and rolling all over the ground. I also cried. The coffin was brought in. I assisted in bathing Yolean's body and in dressing her. The day when I asked Yolean's father to buy her a pair of underwear, he would not. Now when she really did not need them, Yolean's father went and bought a new pair for her, along with a new dress and stockings. At this point I started to cry and told them how sad this was, refusing to buy something for her when she could feel the new things and now putting all of this on her just o be put into the ground. Her father hung his head and walked out.

Yolean was buried the next day in brand new clothes.

16:
Voodoo

What is Voodoo? According to Dr. Jean Price-Mars in his book *Haitian Folkways and Folklore*, "Voodoo is a religion because they believe in the existence of spiritual beings who live somewhere in the universe in close intimacy with human beings. These spiritual beings dominate human activities. It is a religion also because it has priests, a society of followers, temples, altars, ceremonies." It is a mixture of beliefs and rites of African origin, which have been mixed with Catholic practices and it is the religion of the greater part of the peasants and urban people of Haiti.

Voodoo is also a code of living which the Haitians, and most people of African descent in the Americas, use as one of the means at their command to cure sickness, drive away evil forces, and secure a livelihood. The Voodoo religion of Haiti is also practiced in Cuba, Trinidad, Brazil, and the southern United States, especially in Louisiana. Voodoo combines elements of Roman Catholicism and tribal religions of Western Africa, particularly Benin. Voodoo cults worship a high god, called Bon Dieu (good god); ancestors or, more generally the dead; twins; and spirits call Loa. The Loa, which may vary from cult to cult, are African tribal gods that are usually identified with the Roman Catholic saints. The snake god, for example, is identified with St. Patrick. Other elements of Roman

Catholicism in Voodoo include the use of candles, bells, crosses, and prayers with the practices of the baptism and making the sign of the cross. For example, the people are baptized in muddy water with mud. A priest will often have a large black cross when you enter his/her yard. The cross does not symbolize Christ, but is a protection against all evil forces that they do not serve. Among the African elements of Voodoo are dancing, drumming, singing and the worship of the spirits or Loa.

A priest, called a houngan or a priestess, called a mambo, often leads the rituals of Voodoo. During the ritual the worshipers invoke the loa by drumming, dancing, singing and feasting, and the loa takes possession of the dancers. Each dancer then behaves in a manner characteristic of the possessing spirit and while in an ecstatic trance, performs cures and gives advice. Sometimes those in a trance fall to the ground and roll and twist as they are possessed.

L'Attalaye is known for Voodoo. In fact, people come from all over the world to see the local houngan, or witchdoctor, for treatment. For this reason, there are many people who are afraid to come to this part of Haiti. On any given day I could walk the road and see objects of Voodoo in trees, rivers, or lying on the roadside. These items could be chicken heads in bowls, chairs turned upside down in tress, or ropes tied around trees or objects in the river. In the evening in L'Attalaye I could hear the Voodoo drums start to play at about 7 pm. This was a call to the people to their service. There were many houngan who had their own service at that time. These services would last until about 4 am.

I did not know much at all about Voodoo before I arrived, but the women and young girls taught me about many of their beliefs. For example, I learned that the reason no one spoke to me at night was because of their belief that I or anyone could be an evil spirit that took on a familiar facial appearance and if they spoke to me, I could take their spirit. Another belief was that at night all windows had to be closed to keep the evil spirits from coming into the house. No matter how hot it got, the windows stayed closed. The children were not given names at birth because the adults were afraid that if the loa or Spirit knew their children's names, the loa would try to kill them. Many of the children were thus named "Ti gason" (little boy) or "Tifi" (little girl) until they got about two years old.

The people I know say that Voodoo is the worship of God and His helpers. They say that since God is so busy, He needs our help. The helpers are the angels who came from heaven and live in the center of the earth. The people say that there are millions of these helpers, called loa. Each loa has a houngan or witchdoctor that serves him/her. It is thought that what the loa communicates to the houngan is from God.

I am told that each family has a loa that belongs to that family and that one person in the family is gifted or chosen. One of the traditions when a child is born in Haiti (especially in the rural areas), is that a local woman not the mother does certain practices to the child. I observed this in Haiti when assisting with the birth of a baby. Immediately after a baby was born, its mouth is wiped out with garlic to keep the loa from entering the child's mouth. Next, the child is covered with baby powder from head to toe to protect the child from evil spirits. Then the child is taken to the family's local houngan where the family will pay for the witchdoctor's service. The witchdoctor will make a tarry-like concoction of roots and herbs and apply it to the soft spot on the baby's head. The head is then covered with two hats until the child is about two months old. The people believe that this tar substance and covering will prevent an evil spirit from entering the baby's head. Many of the infants had an allergic reaction to this tarry substance. Their scalps broke out in sores and open blisters which of course caused the babies much distress. I had to ask the mothers not to take their babies to the houngan because so many babies were coming to me in the clinic with this problem. It took many months of working with the mothers, but eventually they stopped letting the houngan put the tarry substance on their babies' heads.

In the practices of Voodoo, the people lived in constant fear. I once asked a houngan why the people kept coming back to him. He said "Fear." There are many beliefs that the Haitians practice. When I first came to St. Michel de L'Attalaye, I would sit on my porch and watch the wooden coffins go by. There were daily trips to the Voodoo cemetery just a couple of miles from my house. Sometimes there would be four or even five funerals a day. The people buried their dead in the Voodoo cemetery because they believed that this would keep the houngan from coming at night to get their dead out of the ground and turn them into zombies. The people believed the Voodoo cemetery was safe because there was a legend that once after a baby died a houngan tried to steal the body and turn it into a zombie and the houngan died. People would come from miles around to bury their dead at this particular Voodoo cemetery because of this legend.

The town of L'Attalaye is known all over Haiti as the place to go for good luck. Once a year a town north of L'Attalaye, Ouanaminthe, has a big celebration. People from all over Haiti attend. People come on busses, trucks and even walk. Many mambos, houngans, and worshippers attend wearing the Voodoo colors of red and blue. The color of their clothes represented which loa they served. The loas had names and colors they preferred. To be identified as serving a particular loa was a point of pride, and many people wanted to be easily identified as serving a loa who was identified with the color red. Some wear dresses or pants made of burlap. This is the dress for those who are fasting. This shows that they are humbling themselves before their loa. Some wear belts tied around their waists. The belts are colored red, yellow, white, black or a combination of these colors all representing the different loas. Everywhere there are roosters and chickens of all colors. Each loa likes a different type of rooster or chicken to be used in a sacrifice. People laugh and dance and drink.

Near Carnival time, this group of Voodoo dancers practices the dance for the celebration.

Near the Catholic Church, the people pray to the different statues, for example the Virgin Mary. The people are actually praying to their loa which looks like the Virgin Mary. They often pray in the Catholic churches for their loa to bless them and their families and businesses. Outside of the church there are usually beggars asking for change. People pray in front of a crucifix that hangs outside of a church. Outside of one church I saw Jesus hanging on the cross, but when I got closer I also saw that the people were praying to a houngan who was standing beside the crucifix, and they were paying him as he blessed them. Some people were crying with joy at this, and others were thanking the houngan for blessing them. Still others were there, possessed by their loa.

There is a large, muddy river in town. Along the banks of the river, people have candles and cups of blessed water and they anoint themselves with the water. I was told that this is special water because one of the loa lives in the tree that is in the middle of the large river. In the river there was a man in the mud baptizing the people with the mud. When he finished, they newly baptized were jerking and foaming at the mouth, under the possession of the loa. Later this man himself came under the possession of the loa and he started winding up the tree like a snake.

At the celebration mambos tell each other's fortunes and houngans talk to one another. The people are excited to be in the city. They come every year to receive this special blessing. A lot of this I was able to video. It is a sight I will never forget.

Voodoo is not only a religion in Haiti, but it is a part of their culture. From birth to death, their entire lives are surrounded by Voodoo. In St. Michel you can look in any tree and see a chair turned upside down with a red ribbon tied around the trunk of the tree. This means that some loa live in the tree. The last river that you cross before entering L'Àttalaye is the home of a loa. At many crossroads you can see objects of curses put on someone. You may see a chicken head in a bowl with pennies and corn surrounding it. Just as many times objects meant to curse me were thrown in my yard, there were times people would come to my house at night and perform rituals to send me away. They sang, beat drums, and chanted, but I was protected by God. Voodoo worshippers do not believe in Jesus. As a missionary, I would accompany everything I did with "In the name of Jesus." The only time a Voodoo worshiper says Jesus' name is when they are converted to Christianity.

Many of the towns in Haiti are named after Catholic saints. For example, St. Michel is named after a saint. Each year when the Haitians celebrate St. Michel's birthday, the local Catholic priest blesses the town and right behind him is one of the houngan blessing the town as well. Many people will call the houngan to bless their business when they open a store.

On the radios and some television stations you can hear Voodoo songs being sung. The houngan and pastors, and priests all have some authority over the people, but the houngan have the most power.

The houngans' houses in the rural areas are very distinguished. They are painted with symbols and pictures of the loa that they serve. Some have paintings of snakes, twins, and monster-like creatures. Usually a black cross is painted in front of the entrance to their homes. I once asked why this was so and the houngan told me that "this cross will protect me from the other evil spirits that I don't know or worship." The people believed that the different loas did not get along. They people might get along, but their loas don't so they had to protect themselves from others' loas and even their own loa if they didn't do enough to keep it satisfied. The houngans have red or blue flags on the tops of their houses that can be seen from miles away. This is to let people know where they live if they are needed for service.

Sometimes children are possessed with a loa spirit and people will obey the small children. Once I saw a little girl of about 8 or 9 lead a group of about 50 people. They were going on a fast for their loa. It was amazing to watch them. When the girl would run, they would run. If she walked, they walked. I could see that she was under possession. She seemed to be in some sort of daze.

This girl is believed to be possessed by the spirit of a loa. She visits the clinic with her grandmother.

Once Telese, the local houngan for L'Attalaye, allowed me into his inner sanctuary where he performed his rituals. He had an altar with Moses holding the Ten Commandments and a mambo doll next to Moses. There were many bottles of rum and other bottles containing items I could not identify. The bottles were decorated with jeweled stones and other brightly colored objects. Telese was writing in white chalk on the floor VeVe symbols used in Voodoo practice called VeVe. There were also other items on the floor. There were drums and a pole which ran through the center of the small room to the top of the roof. The people in L'Attalaye told me that this pole was the pole that the loa came through from the center of the earth when they played the drums. The loa would enter the houngan or mambo and possess him/her. I had an opportunity to see this sanctuary because Telese's son was sick and Telese could not get him well. I had helped Telese's daughter deliver a healthy baby boy, and now he wanted me to help his son. The son had a sexually transmitted disease of some sort. I found this out after questioning him about his sexual behavior and his symptoms. I gave him a Cipro for five days and I prayed that Jesus would work through the medication and heal him, and He did. According to Telese though, some other houngan had tried to kill his son because they were jealous of Telese's success as a witchdoctor.

Voodoo is so much a part of the life of a Haitian that is often very difficult for a person coming to Christianity to leave it entirely. I was told by the people who lived in L'Attalaye when I first came to Haiti that people just get sick and die from illness. They believed that when a person got sick, someone was jealous of them or hated them. These people would the go to their houngan and ask the houngan to do something to the person or the person's family who was making them sick. Then, after the person who was sick dies, the family takes revenge for the death of their loved one. And so the revenge would go on and on. In the minds of many of the people, no one dies a natural death and no one gets sick. Instead, someone is putting a curse on them. It is easy to see why they live in fear constantly. This is why, as a missionary, I, along with giving them medicine to get well, I offer Christ, for He will take away all fear so that the Haitian people can live with hope, without fear.

When they go visit the houngan for revenge, the Haitian people have to pay him in cash, land, food, or even sometimes they will sell their children. He will use the children to help him keep his land clean and work them in the gardens. No one goes to a houngan empty-handed for fear he will hurt them.

During Mardi Gras time, there is a group of people called the RaRa band. Each loa has a RaRa band. Each band is led by a houngan dressed in the colors of the loa. The band members too are dressed in the colors of the loa. Someone in the band blows a whistle and snaps the large whip which is used to beat the people they get from the grave as a symbol of control. The horns blow and the people dance in a frenzy, and, like most ceremonies, there is a lot of rum. If the loa lives in a tree, then the rum is poured on the tree. If the loa lives in a rock or a river, rum is poured onto or into that. The houngan and mambo drink a lot of the rum as well. Each band tries to out-dance and out-dress each other. Many of the members are possessed and unaware of what they are doing when they perform. I have seen many people run down and get killed in the road because they will not get out of the way of trucks. The bands start marching on Mardi Gras week and they march every weekend until the week of Easter. The week of Easter they march every night until Good Friday, then all night Friday and Saturday. On that Saturday, in the rural areas, there will be a big celebration and the bands will call out the name of the loa that they are serving. After this final Saturday celebration, the partying is over. I am told that then the bands will sacrifice an animal, usually a chicken, to their loa.

The reason for this RaRa band-led celebration occurring around Easter, I am told, is that the RaRa bands started about the time of Christ, when he was dying on the cross. A group of non-believers started celebrating Christ's death and went off dancing. They did not know that Christ rose from the dead. Because the loas are demons (fallen angels that sinned against God with the devil), they believed that Christ died, and so they celebrated. And so every year the RaRa bands celebrate Christ's death, but not His resurrection. Voodoo worshippers believe in God, but not Jesus Christ, the son of God.

Voodoo is now in the constitution of Haiti as its official religion. It is well known that when Haiti won its independence in 1804 from the French, there was an agreement and a Voodoo service made with the devil to free the Haitians and deliver them from the French. It is said that the very next day after the covenant was made, French blood ran in the streets of Haiti and the people of Haiti were freed.

17:
The Arrest

It was on a Good Friday evening. My husband and I were sitting on the porch of our house in L'Attalaye when suddenly a man approached our gate. He had a gun in his hand and said he wanted to shoot down the guinea hens that were up in one of our trees. He wanted to take them to eat. One of the many things that I learned in Haiti, is that in the evening the hens always go up in a tree for the night. My husband told the stranger not to shoot at the hens because we were sitting on the porch and he might shoot us by accident. The man had been drinking. He refused to listen and proceeded to shoot at the hens in the tree. This made my husband angry. He went to the gate to try and persuade the man to stop. Quickly the discussion got heated and there was a struggle. The man fell, cut his head and started to bleed very badly.

The next thing I knew, dozens of people started to gather at our gate saying that I was a witchdoctor. It all happened so quickly, it really took me by surprise. The people took me and my husband down to a neighboring village, Gethsemee. There they called for the military police. At the time, there was no president in Haiti; the military was running the country. There also had been a lot of kidnappings of pastors and missionaries in Haiti and they were being burned alive, by "necklacing" – putting burning tires around people's necks. When this group of people marched us to the police station, which was really a court in the woods, it was getting dark. The people who insisted that my husband and I go to the woods to the court were some of the very same people we had treated in the clinic. I expected one or two of them to speak on our behalf, but no one did. My husband looked very afraid, but I was not because I knew that somehow God would take care of us.

Earlier in that week I had been reading in the Bible about how God had won the battle for the Israelites simply by confusing their enemies' minds. While all this was happening, I was praying that God would confuse their minds and that we would be set free. The injured man told the people that we were trying to kill him. The military police, called Ton Ton Macute, sat me in a chair in the middle of the large crowd. Some threw dirt in my face. Maybe they thought I would get upset and hurt me that way, but I also saw church members in the crowd who looked worried. I told them I was all right. The military police really enjoyed having an audience. They asked me why I was trying to hurt the man. I did not know that the man was a friend to the military police. At the beginning of our "arrest," I thought maybe we could have been issued a fine and be back home in a few minutes. Little did I know that things would soon get out of hand.

At the time I was a U.S. lieutenant. I was serving in the U.S. Reserves, Nurse Corps and was in Haiti during a break from my service. When I saw that the military police was going to give us over to the crowd which could mean necklacing for both of us, I remembered that I had my military I.D. in my pocket. I knew that the military police did not want to get in trouble with the U.S. by harming an officer in the U.S. army.

By this time it was pitch black. I showed them my military I.D. and one of the police shot his gun in the air to quiet the people. When he saw that I was in the military and was an officer, he stopped the mock trial. He said he had to take us in to town to St. Michel so that the judge could determine our fate. I truly believe that if I had not remembered that I had my I.D. and shown it to them, I would not be alive to tell this tale.

God sure works in mysterious ways. After they saw my I.D., my husband and me were put in a large truck and taken back to town. Our friends in the crowd told us not to get in the truck because they thought we would be driven somewhere and killed. I told them not to worry, and we got in the truck. All the time I was praying.

As the truck left L'Attalaye and headed for St. Michel, the crowd followed and got much larger. I heard the crowd say "Kill them! Kill them!" When we reached town, about three miles away, the crowd had grown to about 1,000. My husband and I were taken to jail, and, since it was 11 pm, there were no judges, so there we stayed. That night, I prayed for safety. I knelt on the dirt floor of the small jail cell and prayed. I prayed like Peter and Paul had prayed when they were in jail. As I was praying, I feared that God did not hear me, but I kept praying. I knew and believed that God will hear His children who are in trouble, for this is what I had read in the Bible for years. My family in the United States had no idea what was happening to me, but my trust and faith were in God.

The next morning I asked if I could make a call home to let my family know what was going on. They allowed me to call, but I could not get through. The phone was in a small building that had two phones and operated on solar panels. If the sun did not shine bright enough to energize the lines, the phone did not work.

Three judges came that afternoon from Gonaives, the large city about two hours south of St. Michel. They heard the evidence presented to them by the injured man. He accused us of having a gun and shooting him. He only had a scalp wound from the tussle with the gun. His family had hired a woman who said she was a nurse, but she was not. She had come earlier to bandage the man's head as he moaned and acted as if he were going to die. When the man finished testifying, the situation got out of hand. The judge wanted to send some military police out to search my house, because we were now suspected of having guns because I was in the military. They accused me of hiding weapons in my house. My prayer remained "Lord, confuse the enemy's mind." They put us back in the truck and took us back to L'Attalaye. They began to search the house and tear up everything – beds were overturned, clothes were pulled out of the closet, pots and pans were pulled out of kitchen cabinets. I knew they wouldn't find anything because there was nothing to find. After they searched the house, they went down to the clinic. There they did the same thing and again found no guns. The police got so disgusted and frustrated one of them asked me for something for his headache, and so I gave him some Tylenol. As they were leaving the clinic, they saw our vegetable garden next to the clinic. They asked for carrots, tomatoes, and onions, and of course, we gave them whatever vegetables they wanted. We then returned to town.

The police told the judge that they found no guns. The judge sent us before two more judges. They could not find any evidence that we had done anything wrong. We were then sent back to the first judge who finally allowed me to talk. I told him how disappointed I was with the people in town because I had only come to Haiti to help them, not hurt them. The judge apologized for his people, but he made me pay the "nurse" who bandaged the man's head. I shook hands with my accuser and told him that I was not mad at him. I knew in my heart that all the chaos was not his fault. I was later told that the houngan had told the people to cause a disturbance against me. The houngan reasoned that I would leave St. Michel, and he and the other houngans could have the people back to themselves. When the "trial" was over, I walked onto the porch of the courthouse and began to cry. I knew I was fighting something greater than the people and me. I knew that I had what they needed and that others didn't want the people to have my help. What I had was help for both the natural and spiritual. I offered a better way of life - a life without fear, and a life filled with joy.

The day after we were released from jail, I went right back to the clinic to work. All that day at the clinic felt like a victory for Jesus and for me. The devil thought he got me, but I got away with the help of God. Some of the same people who had accused me of being a witchdoctor and caused the arrest and all the chaos were on the porch waiting to be seen. And because of love, they were treated.

18:
He Will Provide

Many times God provided me with what I needed while I was living in L'Attalaye. One such time God's blessing was the arrival of a few small mice.

I had been to Port-au-Prince to check my mailbox. As usual, there were no checks or money in the letters. I received many letters telling me "God will provide," and sometimes these letters contained a donation. But for this trip to town I had only enough money to put enough gas in the jeep to make the trip to the mailbox and back. When I arrived in St. Michel, I had no cash and none of the letters contained any donation, so I asked one of the pastors in town if he could loan me ten dollars. He told me no which was disappointing because I had helped him at my clinic. I headed for home feeling sad. It was pitch black dark. I could not see behind me or in front of me. The moon was just a sliver, so I was driving along on the dark, bumpy road I could barely follow. I finally made it home.

In my bedroom I had a closet. I had the closet made when we renovated the house. The closet had no light. I really didn't like going in there, but when I did I would make a noise to scare the mice away. I've always been afraid of mice, not because of what they might do, but because they jump and run so suddenly. At night I could hear mice scratching and chewing. I imagined them having the sharpest teeth imaginable. One time when I left an open can of peanut butter on the kitchen table, I found their tiny paw prints in it in the morning! I even slept under tightly tucked covers because the mice would sometimes jump on the bed! Many times I got poison to kill them, but I never really got rid of them. Sometimes before I entered the closet, I'd throw a shoe inside to scare away the mice.

The morning after my trip to St. Michel for my mail, Marie the housekeeper came to clean. I was still sad because I had no money, but I continued to believe that God would see me through. Marie started cleaning my bedroom and was moving to sweep out the closet. Like me, she threw a shoe in the closet to scare away the mice. This time the mice jumped out and one had a small brown, rolled-up object in its mouth. The mice scattered but left the brown object and I heard Marie call me. She had picked up the brown roll and handed it to me. I hesitated to take it because I could see the teeth marks from the mice. I carefully unrolled the paper and inside I found thirty dollars! I couldn't believe it. Apparently I had misplaced the money some time ago. I laughed because I saw that God had used the mice to bring it to me!

Another time when my husband and I went to Port-au-Prince to check our mail, I again found that no one had sent any money. This time I didn't even have enough gas money to get back to St. Michel. The distance to St. Michel from Port-au-Prince is about 3 miles. After I checked my mail, my husband and I visited an American missionary whom I had met a couple of years before and who was currently staying in

Port-au-Prince. Her name was Sister Lee and she came from New Jersey. She did not live in Haiti, but would come four or five times a year and give food to schools and churches. She was 75 years old at the time. She had a house not far from the airport, so I decided to visit her there. Luckily she was home, but she was not alone. She had visitors from Bermuda, a pastor and his wife, who had come to see Sister Lee's work in Haiti. Sister Lee introduced me and my husband to her friends who asked us what kind of work we did in Haiti. We ate lunch together and then it was time to go. Sister Lee always brought back a little food from the States for me when she came back to Haiti. Sister Lee gave me the care package, and the wife of the pastor shook my hand. I felt her give me money when she shook my hand and my heart rang for joy. Once again God had provided.

When we got into the jeep, I told my husband that God had provided us with money to get us back to St. Michel. After we had gotten out of view, I opened my purse to see how much money the pastor's wife had given me. The money was in a roll and the first bill was $100! I cried with joy, and then I pulled back another bill which was another $100 and then another and another until I was holding $500! When I exchanged the $500 U.S. dollars, I had over $2,500 of Haitian dollars. We had enough money to buy food, gas, and do some repairs on the jeep which had an oil leak. That day God made a way for us by using strangers all the way from Bermuda. God will provide even if He has to bring it from hundreds of miles away.

Yet another time I was in Port-au-Prince once again with no money. I had spent my last two dollars for a cab to visit my friend Ruth, another missionary in Haiti. When I got in the taxi, I knew I had given the driver less than what he required. Then suddenly I felt God tell me to look on the floor of the taxi and there I saw a dirty $5 bill. This was enough to get me to Ruth's house where I knew she could help me further. Even in the poorest country in the Western hemisphere, even in the mouth of a mouse, or from hundreds of miles away or hidden in a cab, God will provide.

19:
The Rivers

My husband and I had left Port-au-Prince late one morning. Milfort was driving our small blue jeep. We were trying to get to St. Michel before the rain started for we knew that if the rain started before we got to the halfway point, Gonaives, then the 13 rivers would flood and we would not be able to cross the rivers until the flooding subsided. Sometimes this took one or two days.

By the time we reached Gonaives it was raining. We looked over the mountains towards St. Michel and saw more dark rain clouds. When we reached Ennery, the town where Louverture was born, the first river was beginning to flood. My husband did not want to cross, but I knew we had to get home. He drove the jeep into the river in the middle of the roaring, gushing water. The jeep stopped and went into a dive into the river. I looked to my left and saw more water rushing toward my window. The engine stalled and I yelled "Jesus!" with all the might and power in my body. My husband turned the key in the ignition and the engine started. I felt like someone was pulling on the back of the jeep even though we didn't see anyone. Immediately the jeep was out of the river. What a miracle! Mud was inside the jeep and we were both soaking wet, but we were okay!

We kept going to the next large river. It too was flooded. By this time it was pitch black, but there was some moonlight. There was no one on the road but God, us and the river rushing down from the higher mountains with such force that it had torn down large trees. I told my husband to stop the jeep. I got out and saw that a large tree had blocked out passage. I prayed and asked God what to do. He said "Get out of the jeep and get into the river and push the tree out of your way." I told my husband what I was going to do and he said "You must be crazy." Nevertheless, my husband waded out to join me and we both got into the rushing river holding each other's hand and waded toward the fallen mango tree. We gave it one push and it went swiftly down the river as if a much greater force than ourselves had shoved it into the strong current. All it takes is a little bit of faith. Step out for God and He will do the rest.

We returned to the jeep, prayed a prayer of thanks, and then Milfort started the jeep once again and we started across the river. It took us many hours to cross the other 11 rivers. Some were easy to cross, others were much more difficult with slippery banks we had to repeatedly climb and slip down, but finally God brought us all the way home.

The next morning I was sure the engine of the jeep would not work. Mud had filled the engine. But, when I turned the key and said a little prayer, it turned on and hummed. I thought of the night before and thought that God always keeps His promises. I may be in rough waters, enough to drown me, but God said "It will not overtake you." That night His words truly came true.

Milfort and me by the jeep that got us through the rivers.

20:
The Mark

I have read many stories about missionaries all over the world, and one of the most common threads about most of them is that they all have some kind of mark on their body that says they've served as missionaries. I have read stories of missionaries who have been burned on one of their arms or legs. Others have been cut so severely they will die with this mark. Others have even lost limbs, or an eye. One story I read told of a missionary who served in Africa. He had been severely burned on his right arm. One day he was out in the jungle and a lion attacked and killed him. The lion ate or mauled all of his body. The only identifiable sign was a right arm that had a bad burn scar on it. This was the only thing left of his body, the only mark by which his family could identify him.

When I came to Haiti in 1988 to work full time as a missionary, I received my mark. While working in Cite Soleil, something bit me on my left forearm. I do not know what insect bit me, maybe a mosquito or some other bug. For many days the raised area on my arm itched and burned and turned red. There were two pinpoint bites in the middle of the raised bump. It would not stop itching no matter what I put on it. After several weeks, the bump dried up and turned black. By this time the two small bites had increased to the size of two small dimes.

When I returned home I went to an infectious disease doctor. He was unable to diagnose what had bitten me. It has been almost 18 years and I still have those two spots on my arm. Many people have asked me what it's from and I always say it's my mark.

21:
The Fire

I had just finished painting the inside of the house in L'Attalaye. The rooms had been painted different colors. The sitting room was yellow, the living groom was orange, the bedrooms were off-white, the kitchen was yellow and the bathroom orange. All of the rooms had furniture that had been made from Mahogany trees or that I had purchased in Port-au-Prince. The sitting room was the room you saw when you first entered the house. It had furniture made out of wicker, a sofa, a large chair and a small cocktail table. I had purchased quite a bit of Haitian art and it was hanging on the walls. I had pictures of my family on the bookcase. The living room had two large bookcases built in to the walls. They had over 200 books of all types. Our bedroom had a small bed, a dresser, and a closet. There were pictures on the walls there too, and I had even brought a rug from the States to put on the floor. We had no doors on the rooms, so I hung colorful curtains to match the color of the walls. The guest room had two small twin beds and a small dresser. The kitchen was in the back of the house. It had cabinets, and a sink. Even though we did not have running water, the sink was nice to have. I had purchased the stove and used a Butane gas tank. I had a small table built with four chairs made from Mahogany trees. Just across from the kitchen was the bathroom. We had a toilet, bathtub and tiled walls and floor. We got water from the well and poured it into the toilet and tub. All the windows had screens to keep out the bugs. I even had a screen door made so the cool air could blow from the front yard all the way through the house and out the back door. Truly our house was a home.

Here I am by my rows of okra, part of my large vegetable garden at my home in L'Attalaye in 1989.

The front yard had large tropical flowers and four large Mahogany trees. I always had a garden with vegetables growing. Our home could be seen by people as they traveled on their way to and from the market. It was our little paradise. It was especially appreciated after coming home from a long trip to Port-au-Prince. By this time we also had a vehicle, our jeep that was given to us by the Mission Department. Life was good.

When I first came to Haiti, life was very difficult. I was living with different families, I didn't have much to eat and I had to bathe in the rivers. I had to ride public transportation often sleeping with strangers which was often not very comfortable or clean. In nine years, my life in Haiti had changed dramatically. I had a little radio, and, as long as I had batteries, I could listen to music which I really loved. The house and the gardens were beautiful to Milfort and me. Even though we did not have electricity or running water, life was still much better for me than when I first arrived as a missionary in 1988.

It was in April, 1997. The yard was in full bloom. The yard had been transformed into a beautiful oasis. There were several banana trees on the side, ferns were planted all around the house and several tall, shady trees had been planted in the back. The coconut tree out front was growing, the flower garden had zinnias, poppies, and other tropical flowers of bright colors. The vegetable garden had tomatoes, onions, okra and cabbage. I always had enough food to eat. People brought me food daily to the clinic because they had no money to pay. The people brought whatever fruit or vegetable was in season. I had plenty of tomatoes, carrots, onions, bananas, pineapples, and grapefruit. Everything seemed to finally be falling into place. I hardly had any worries.

By this time, my mail was coming to the mailbox in Petionville, much closer than Port-au-Prince. I always had a little money. I was seeing about 80-100 people a day by myself at the clinic. While this seems like a lot, I was treating the symptoms. There was no testing done. If they had a headache, I gave them Tylenol. If they had an upset stomach, I gave them Pepto-Bismol. If they had some type of infection,

I gave them antibiotics. If the children had worms, they got medicine for that. If they had some complaint that I could not treat, I prayed. If they did not get better, they died. I had found a rhythm, a way not just to survive in Haiti, but a way to be happy. All seemed to be going well. And then came the fire.

It came one evening while I was at church up the road in L'Attalaye. That day I had worked in the clinic all day and was tired. I had eaten dinner and was preparing to go to bed. My husband came and asked me to go to church with him. After much hesitation I said yes. Usually I would have taken a bath and changed my clothes, but that evening I didn't feel like it, so I went to church not very clean.

It was getting to be dusk, so I lit the kerosene lamps and put a candle in the bathroom tub for light. I also put a candle in the kitchen sink. This is what I always did when I left for church service at night. The candles were not near any curtains. I left home about 6:45 pm. It was dark. The church was about a quarter of a mile away.

While in church I felt like getting up and leaving two or three times, but a small voice said "Wait." And so I waited. I was very tired and dirty. Church services ended at 7:30pm. When I came outside, I saw a large blazing fire. This was not unusual. During planting season the people burned their fields to destroy old corn husks. But as we approached the fire we realized that it was not a field on fire, but our house! Flames were shooting out the windows, doors and tin roof. People had gathered on the road and were screaming and hollering and crying with great grief. Some of the women had thrown themselves on the ground and were rolling around in the dirt screaming with grief. There was a large truck parked in front of the house safely away from the fire, and some young men near the truck were acting suspiciously. My jeep was still parked along the side of the house. As I looked at the fire that was consuming my beautiful little home I heard a small voice again say to me "It's just a test." I did not get upset or cry, but instead thanked God for my life. One of the young men came running to me and said "Give me the key to the jeep!"

I had forgotten that I had the key to the jeep in my pocket. But, somehow, God would not let me give the young man the key. Instead, I got into the jeep and backed it out onto the road and continued to watch the fire engulf my home. I stood there watching the fire knowing there was no water to put it out, no fire truck to call. All my memories of all the people I had met in Haiti and the books, music cassettes, photographs of my family, Bibles, my passport, my airplane ticket and my money were burning up with my house. Me, my husband and all the people I had helped in the area all stood and watched the fire. But this time the large truck that was suspiciously out of harm's way had left and was on its way toward St. Raphael, probably filled with all the items the young men had stolen before they set fire to the house.

I will never forget the kindness of the people of L'Attalaye. When they realized that I had lost everything in the fire, they went to their little huts and began to give me items from their homes. Everything equal or similar to everything I had lost in the fire they replaced. Some gave me clothes, shoes, a towel. Others gave me food such as eggs, oil, onions and a skillet to cook with. Still others gave me deodorant, shampoo, and cologne. They gave me a mattress, sheets and a pillow. When I had all this, a woman said "Here is some money." She gave me all she had: $1.00. God had replaced everything I had lost in the fire.

The next morning they all marched down the road with me to the clinic. The house was still smoking, but the flames were out. I set up house in the clinic and thanked them and God. Then they all left and went back to their huts. Even my husband left me and went back to St. Michel! I was all alone, except for Jesus.

The next morning as I returned to the house, it was still smoking. There was nothing, absolutely nothing left. All the furniture was totally burned up. Even the furniture that had a metal frame was gone. All the paint had burned off the walls. There were no doors, no cabinets, no windows. While I walked through I found the nails that had once held the furniture together. The tile in the bathroom had buckled. Even the tin roof had been destroyed, but I was grateful to be alive.

Later that week I learned that my neighbor had heard someone in the house right before the fire started. She did not go to my house because, like so many Haitians, she did not go outside in the dark. She was afraid of the men. She said that they had a gun. I don't know if this is true or not. Some say a witchdoctor set the fire. Only God really knows who set the fire. All I knew was that the fire came and 12 years went up in flames, but I did not.

The day after the fire I was sitting on the porch of the clinic feeling very much alone. I felt my labor and hard work was for nothing. I felt like the loneliest person in the world. I felt as if there was no one to comfort me, no one to hug me, no one to say "Everything is all right." I felt as if I had no family or friend in the world. It was just me, sitting on a cement step, still smelling like smoke, my dirty hair uncombed, just totally alone.

In the distance I heard a group of people singing. They were singing "He Promises to Never Leave You Alone" in Creole. I knew a mission group was coming to L'Attalaye, but I thought they were going to visit someone else, but as they approached the clinic, they turned into the gate. They kept singing "No never alone, no never alone, He promises never to leave you alone." This was a song I was familiar with.

The world's fierce winds are blowing,
Temptation's sharp and keen
I have a peace in knowing
My Savior stands between
He stands to shield me from danger
When earthly friends are gone
He promised never to leave me
Never to leave me alone.
No never alone
No never alone
He promised never to leave me
Never to leave me alone.

It was then that I realized they were singing to me. God had sent them all the way from town to encourage me. They prayed for me and left singing "No Never Alone." My heart was lifted and encouraged. I no longer felt alone.

After the mission group left, I looked toward down the road toward the next small town after L'Attalaye, and saw a man riding toward me on a bicycle. He came into the yard with a white envelope. He gave it to me and said "It's not much, but maybe it will help." When I opened the envelope it was filled with money. When I counted it, it was $350 Haitian. I just praised and thanked God. Now I had enough money to go to Port-au-Prince to get another passport. Not only did this man give me money, he also gave me a sack of vegetables. Just as quickly as he appeared on his bicycle, he drove out of the gate and left. I never saw him again. I never even learned his name. God kept His promise to me. He never left me alone. I was really never alone!

After arriving in Port-au-Prince, I was able to get a passport, call home to get another airplane ticket and additional money. My heart was no longer discouraged or defeated. God spared my life and provided means for me to replace what the fire had destroyed.

1997 was the year the house burned and the year I left St. Michel. I still return to Haiti several times a year, but I work now at Carrefour where Pastor Vilyo lets me use his church to set up a clinic. As of yet, the house has not been rebuilt, but when I return to Haiti I know that God is still in control and I also know that God loves people everywhere, even in the poorest places of the world. Maybe one day the house will be rebuilt. The fire destroyed my material substance, but it didn't destroy my memories or me!

I stand in front of what is left of my home in L'Attalaye. The walls are the only part still intact.

My once beautiful garden as it is today. The Mahogany trees have been cut down for charcoal and cows have long since trampled the vegetable garden. The burned house stands to the right.

22:
Haiti

I have been working in Haiti as a medical missionary for over 34 years. When I first came to Haiti, I did not like the country or the people, but I asked God to put love in my heart. I thought I was going to be preaching the Gospel to these people, and that they would be saved. I had no intention of just allowing God to use me as He saw fit. I soon learned that God had other plans for me, and that one of the biggest changes that occurred was in me. My love for both Haiti and its people will be with me forever.

My husband, Milfort, as I affectionately called him, was a great help and influence on me while I worked in Haiti. We met in the U.S. in 1986 while he was looking for someone to help him work in a clinic he wanted to build in his homeland of Haiti. I agreed to work with him and together we worked very hard. Sometimes we worked together as a team, and sometimes we worked independently of one another. Milfort was Haitian and it was his desire to help his people and to inspire them to help themselves. He built many churches and schools along with building a home with me in L'Attalaye. Milfort taught me how to drive in the mountains of Haiti, and how to drive in the mud without getting stuck. He helped me learn Creole and how to be stronger with the Haitians.

On December 5, 2014 when I was back in the States and Milfort was in Haiti, I received a call from

Haiti at about 7 pm that Milfort had died. He had gone to Haiti to see his family. Milfort had many chronic illnesses. He had diabetes, heart disease, hypertension and had received a kidney transplant three years prior, and he was blind in one eye. He was told by all of his doctors in the U.S. not to return to Haiti for health reasons, but he always insisted on going. For the last several years, when Milfort went home to Haiti and I could not go with him, he would get sick. I would then meet him at the airport in Detroit and would take him straight to the hospital. This time he did not make it back to me in time.

I went back to Haiti to bury Milfort. This was very difficult. Not only did I lose him, I also found out that he had been in a coma before he died. He also died in St.Michel de L'Attalaye, where we worked. My dear friend Ruth met me at the airport in Haiti along with Pastor. We drove to St. Michel de L'Attalaye. The bumpy drive through the rough mountains and through the 13 rivers brought back so many memories. I thought about the many times Milfort and I had driven these roads through the night, trying to get home. Many times we were the only car on the road. I thought about the time we almost drowned in the 12 rivers. I thought about the food we would eat on the way home, the sweet bananas and peanut butter sandwiches, the mangoes, fried chicken feet, and cold Coke. As we drove I thought about how I would never hear Milfort's voice again. I had no family with me to console me or even give me a simple hug. Again I had to lean on God. I had much to do once I arrived in St. Michel. First I had to identify the body and then I had to arrange the funeral. Through all of this I heard God say to me: "I am with you. I will not leave you." God gave me the strength to complete everything that needed to be done. When we arrived in St. Michel, I noticed that some things had changed in the years I had been coming. They now had a gas station. There were more cars, lots of motorcycles, and they had a high school and two funeral homes. Many of the houses had solar systems providing electricity. Part of the dirt road had been paved. The people drank purified water.

Here I am with my waiting patients in Croix de Bouchet in Port-au-Prince.

The clinic in Croix de Bouchet west of Port-au-Prince has a tin roof which offers no relief from the blazing heat.

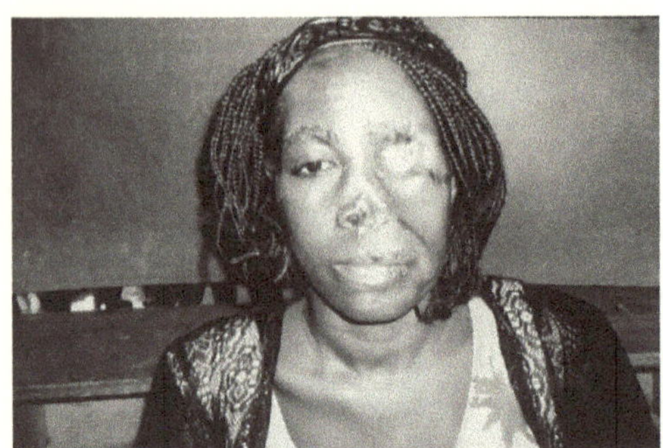

This woman was badly injured in the hurricane of 2010. She is hoping to get reconstructive surgery, but has no money. She has twins and difficulty breathing. It is very unlikely that she will get the surgery.

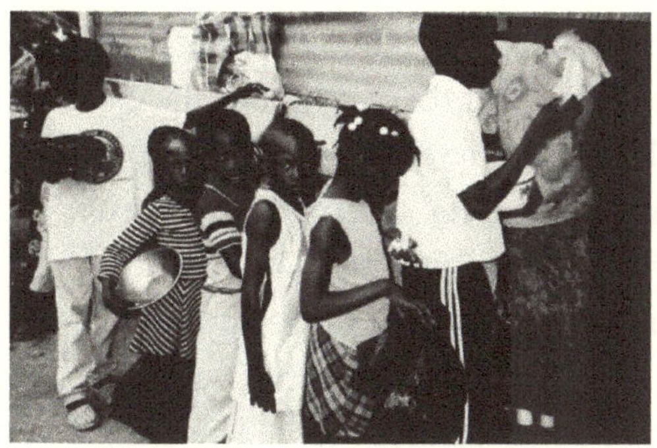

Children line up outside of the clinic for rice and beans. Money was donated for the rice and beans – a pleasant an infrequent surprise.

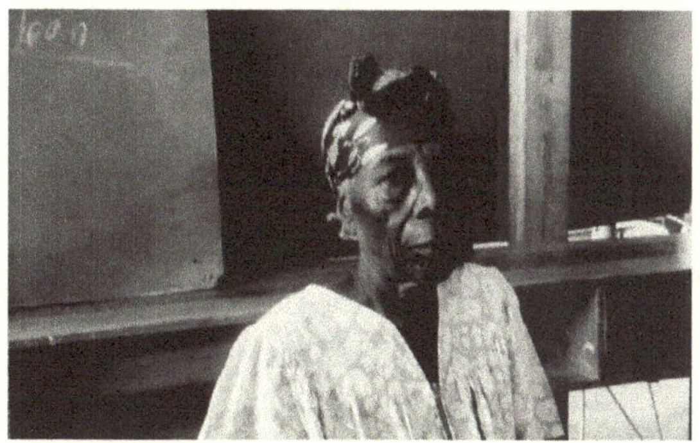

As a woman in her 80s, this patient is very unusual. The life expectancy in Haiti is 52.

Some things, though, remained the same. The people still lived in poverty, still much worse than Port-au-Prince. The pastor was Haitian, but he had never been to St. Michel de L'Attalaye. He had never seen such poverty or the practice of Voodoo. He was shocked. He told me that "God must have sent you to this place" because of its suffering. There was evidence of Voodoo all around, in the trees, on the ground at crossroads. L'Attalaye was still a dusty and dry place. People still lived in huts. But as we drove through the town, I began to remember so much. What was left of our burned out house was still there, without the flowers and trees. There was saw a cow tied up in the yard. It brought tears to my eyes. I remembered how Milfort would sit outside at night and look up at the beautiful stars, or how we would sit on the porch when it rained and listen to the sound. And then I saw the clinic. There were not many people there. The people said they were waiting for me to return. I remembered the days when people from miles around would come to the clinic and I would see 100 people a day. I remembered the ones who got better and the ones who died in my arms. I saw the church Milfort had built across from our home. The church was still active and had a new pastor.

I buried Milfort on December 18, 2014. He had a grand funeral, just like the ones they have in New Orleans. He had a grey metal casket with many flowers. He was buried in his black suit. There was a band, singing and a hearse was driven through town for all the people to see.

I came to Haiti 34 years ago thinking I was going to change Haiti, but Haiti changed me. Haiti changed me into a humble, compassionate person for whom Haiti and its people will always be dear.

At the clinic in Croix de Bouchet in Port-au-Prince.

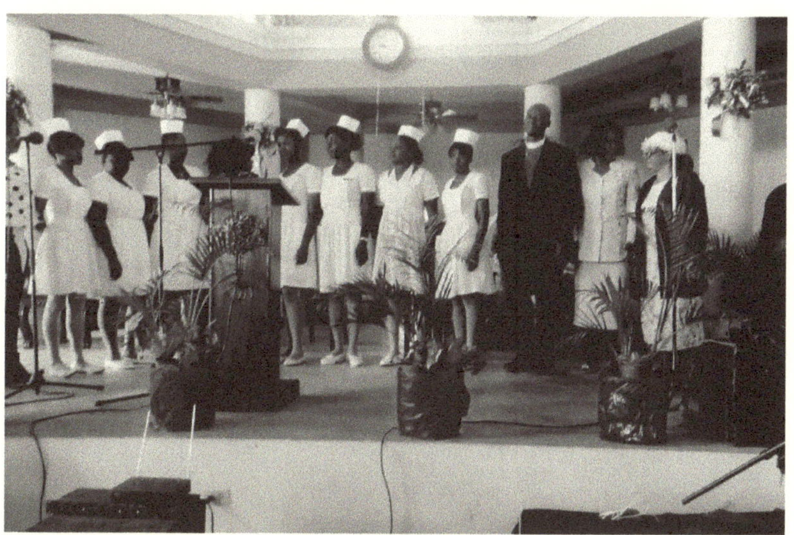

This group of nursing students has finished their first year of nursing school offered by a church. After another year they will be RNs. My hope is that they will stay in Haiti.

Acknowledgments:

Much of the information regarding Haiti and Voodoo I learned after and during my stay there and from Lyonel Paquin's *The Haitians: Class and Color Politics* and Jean Price-Mars' *Haitian Folkway and Folklore*.